MT. ST. HELENS
The Volcano Explodes!

MT. ST. HELENS

The Volcano Explodes!

Prof. Leonard Palmer

and KOIN-TV Newsroom (6), Portland, Oregon

NORTHWEST Illustrated

ISBN: 0-86519-004-6 Paperback
0-86519-005-4 Collector's Edition

Designed by Irene Friedman

Printed in The United States of America

This book is dedicated to the men
who lost their lives collecting data
on the slopes of Mt. St. Helens:

Reid Blackburn

Dave Johnson

Bob Kaseweter

Bob Landsburg

Gerald Martin

Table of Contents

Illustration Acknowledgements

John Allen — 152.

© Thomas J. Atiyeh — 114.

Maury Dahlen/KOIN — 7.

Tom Gleason/KOIN — 20,32,58,59,173,192.

Paul Hammond — 49.

John Keller/KOIN — Title Page,25,26, 27,28,29,31,133,134,160,161, 162,163,164,165,166,167,168,169,170,171, 172,180,186,187,190,193.

KOIN-TV Syndicated Video Tape — 9,10,87, 88,89,90,108,109,110,111,112,113,141,146, 147,148,153,154,155,157,159,189, 191,196.

NAPP Systems (USA) INC. — 142,143,144, 145.

© Leonard Palmer — 13,14,15,16,17,18,19, 21,22,23,24,34,35,36,37,38,39,40,41,42,43,44, 45,46,47,48,50,51,52,53,54,55,56,57,60,61,62, 63,64,65,66,67,68,69,70,71,72,73,74,75,76,77, 78,79,80,81,82,83,84,85,86,115,116,117,118, 119,120,121,122,123,124,125,126,127,128, 129,130,131,132,135,136,137,138,139,140, 149,150,151,156,158,174,175,176,177, 178,179,181,182,183,184,185,188.

© 1980 Robert Rogers — 100,101,102,103,104, 105,106,107.

© Gary Rosenquist/Earth Images — 92,93,94, 95,96,97,98,99.

Mick Schafbuch/KOIN — 33.

Mike Slowik/KOIN — 194,195.

Chris Thoms — 2,3,4,5,6.

Ken Woo/KOIN — 30.

Prologue
The Legend of Loo-wit

The Indian tribes of the Columbia River each have a legend about the creation of Mt. St. Helens. One version tells of two sons of the Great Spirit and the beautiful young maiden they both loved.

For many years the two chiefs and their people lived in peace with one another and visited each other across the bridge the Great Spirit had created for that purpose over the wide river. When they eventually became selfish, greedy, and quarrelsome, the Great Spirit punished them by taking away the sun. When winter came, they had no fire to keep warm and they grew sorry and prayed to the Great Spirit for fire to keep from dying from the cold. His heart softened by their prayers, the Great Spirit went to an old woman who was free of any wrongdoing and still had fire in her lodge. If she would share her fire with the people, the Great Spirit told her, he would grant her most fervent wish. She agreed to take her fire to the bridge and keep it burning always for the people on both sides of the river. When asked what she most desired, the old woman, whose name was Loo-wit, asked to be young and beautiful.

In the morning Loo-wit, once again young and beautiful, was found at the Bridge of the Gods, as it was known, with fire to warm the lodges of both tribes. The sun shone again and all lived in peace and harmony. This was not to last. Loo-wit's beauty was such that the two chiefs, Wyeast from one side of the river, Klickitat from the other, fell deeply in love with her and wanted her to choose between them. She cared for them equally and could not decide between them. They grew jealous and angry and fought. Their people fought as well and there were many deaths. The Great Spirit himself was so angered by these events that he destroyed the Bridge of the Gods, the sign of peace between the two tribes, and transformed the chiefs into mountains. Wyeast became Mt. Hood; Klickitat, Mt. Adams.

Loo-wit was also punished — she too became a mountain. The Great Spirit promised her even though he must punish her with a long, icy sleep, she would still be beautiful.

Loo-wit became the beautiful, snow-capped mountain known as Mt. St. Helens.

INTRODUCTION

In a land built by volcanoes, stories of mountains prevail. This has always been so. Traditional tales of the Northwest Indians focused most particularly on mountains — on their creation, their destruction, on the lakes and rivers produced by volcanic activity, and on the gods, demons, and mortals who played their part in mythical accounts of volcanic eruptions.

Most residents of the Northwest know the story of Loo-wit, restored by the Great Spirit to youth and beauty, and then transformed into Mt. St. Helens when Wyeast and Klickitat, two chiefs who became Mt. Hood and Mt. Adams, resorted to battling for her favor. In such ways the Indians explain the multiple eruptions of three volcanic peaks which today surround the city of Portland, Oregon. By doing so, the Indians brought into human perspective what is otherwise beyond our comprehension, for rivalry, even on a mountain-size scale, is a concept human beings can readily understand.

There are other tales. In one, the chief who battles the mountain spirits by flinging rocks down their crater, collapses in despair when he sees his land is destroyed. In his defeat he is buried by molten rock and remains forever part of Mt. Hood.

In yet another tale, the chief of the aboveworld defeats the chief of the underworld by bringing down the top of the mountain we call Mt. Mazama and creating in the process the body of water known today as Crater Lake.

In all the Indian tales of volcanic eruptions, the human element dominates; and yet, stripped of their mythical features, stripped of their demon, their larger than life chiefs and warriors, these stories ring true. The trembling Earth, the ice that falls like rain, the glowing rock, the fire

that rolls down the mountainside are not merely bits of legend in the tales of a primitive people, but a vivid reality to those who lived near to Mt. St. Helens.

The term volcano dates back even further than Indian legend to Roman mythology. Vulcan, one of the three children of Jupiter and Juno, was considered to be the god of fire and blacksmith to the gods. Vulcan's workshop could be identified by various active volcanoes, each "smoking mountain" being nothing less than the chimney of Vulcan's forge. Vulcan was regarded by mere mortals as a god of destructive force and his forge was said to be on the island of Vulcano, off the coast of Sicily. Hence the word volcano, derived from the Latin Vulcanus or Volcanus — the names given the island in ancient times.

Legends aside, since the dawn of recorded time, man has had ample and continuing cause to marvel at the awesome might — and mystery — of volcanoes. They have been natural agents of some of the most terrible destruction ever wrought on mankind.

What is perhaps the most famous volcanic eruption in history, that of Mt. Vesuvius in 79 A.D., produced a death toll estimated in the thousands. Pompeii remains today a preserved artifact created by the ash fallout from that volcanic event. A second eruption there in 1691 left no

Mt. Vesuvius, 1631.

such monument to history but was almost certainly more lethal, with more than 3,000 known deaths.

Mt. Etna, 1865.

In 1729 the eruption of nearby Sicily's Mt. Etna, Europe's largest volcano, was of such calamitous proportions that at least 20,000 people perished. Unhappily even this staggering figure was exceeded several times in more recent years. The eruption of Indonesia's Tambora, in 1815, caused an estimated 66,000 deaths; in the wake of the volcano known as Krakatoa, also in Indonesia, in 1883, there were an estimated 96,000 victims. These were two of the more staggering in terms of fatalities.

At the same time — and there is the paradox — volcanoes have afforded great pleasure to man in their role as awe-inspiring giants of the physical world. Some of the loftiest, most spectacular mountains on the face of this earth are volcanic cones. Even when erupting there is extraordinary beauty in their terrible force and power. They have the ability to transform the sky; to produce sunsets of strong, almost unearthly color combinations.

Like the chief defeated by the mountain spirits, area residents look out and see a land that was once green and living now utterly and completely devoid of life. Trees and animals gone, and the rivers choked with the flooding debris. Mt. St. Helens, the mountain that they call their own, is not a permanent feature in the landscape, but rather a manifestation of a process — a living, growing, dying and regenerating process — which scientists tell us has happened time and again in geological history of the Northwest.

1
A VOLCANO IS NOT JUST A TALL MOUNTAIN

Popular Misconceptions About Volcanoes

You cannot always see a volcano. There are volcanoes under the sea and under glaciers.

Volcanoes do not emit smoke and fire. No burning in the sense of combustion is taking place. The so-called fire is really the reflection of the red-hot materials *inside* the volcano upon the volcanic cloud *above* it. The cloud itself — the "smoke" we hear so much about — is composed of gases and vapor (condensed steam) and dust-ash particles. The color of this eruptive cloud depends on the relative amount of dust-ash and incandescent material in it. When it is dark and forbidding, there is much much more dust-ash content; when it seems luminous and almost glowing, there is much more of the incandescent materials.

Nineteenth century interpretation of Stromboli eruption, 1825.

Volcanoes do not always literally blow their tops. As often as not, the eruption takes place through craters on the side. For that matter, the volcano creates craters wherever it happens to erupt through the surface of the mountain. An existing crater may just happen to be the path of least resistance and be the site of a new eruption.

Every volcano does not have a river of lava rushing down its sides. This notion reflects movie epics of the 30's and 40's more than it does the workings of nature.

What is a volcano then? A volcano is at once one of the most complex — and elemental — of Earth's processes.

How Volcanoes Are Formed

A volcano is formed when hot molten rock from inside the earth, called magma, erupts and creates a new part of the Earth's surface. Magma may boil up from the ocean floor to form new islands or blast debris and even pour lava — the word commonly used for molten rock flowing out of the earth — upon the land near it. It can also create undersea mountains.

Volcanoes are very special kinds of mountains in that they sustain the continuing primeval process which originally generated the surface of the Earth. This process from time immemorial is continuing today and will never cease to continue.

Volcanic eruptions are an essential source of life-sustaining conditions on Earth. They have segregated water from rock material and thus formed the atmosphere and hydrosphere of our Earth, the blue planet. These processes are violent, but they are a prime source of life, the beginning from which the oceans and continents were formed.

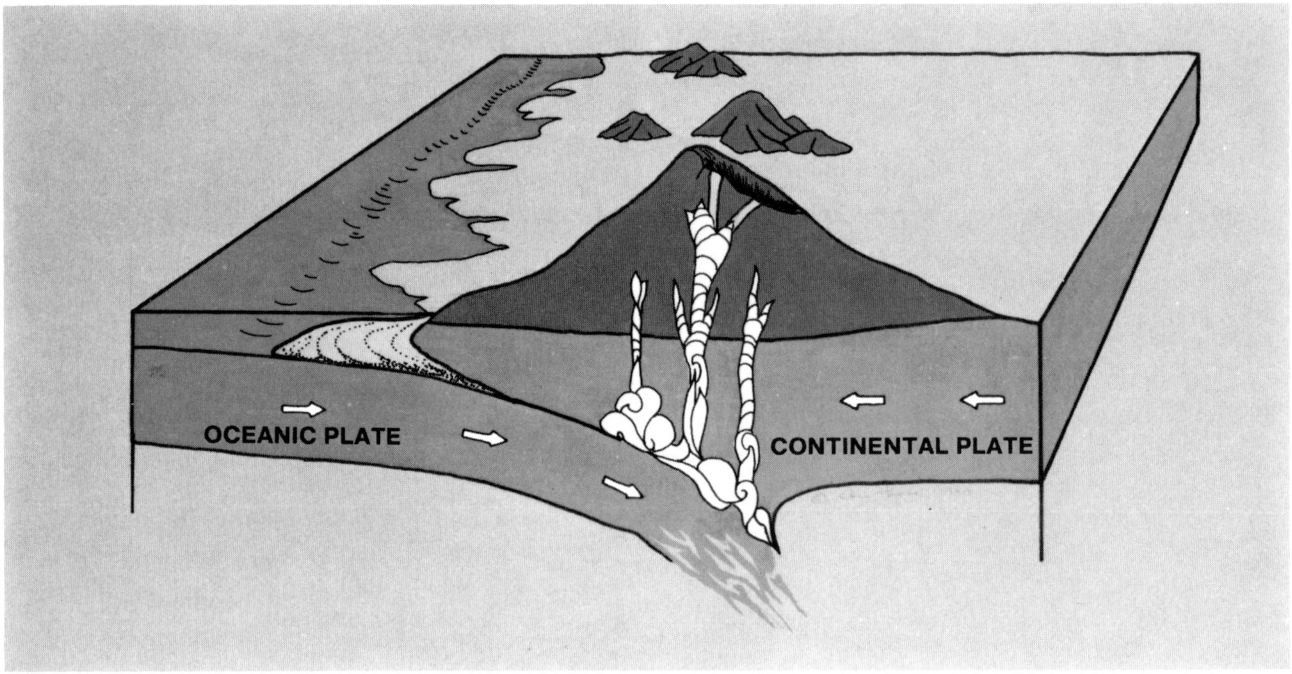

Illustration of the coming together of the oceanic and continental plates causing the formation of a volcano.

2.

Where Does Magma Come From?

The origin of the magma is from deep within the crust of the Earth. Most volcanoes form where two rigid slabs of the Earth's crust (called plates) meet. They may be pulling apart or pushing together or sliding sideways. The magma leaks through weaknesses near these boundaries.

In the Pacific Northwest, at the boundary between the oceanic and continental plates, the composition of the magma is changed by incorporation of material reworked from older continental geological units. This is why Mt. St. Helens is more dangerous than Hawaiian volcanoes. In the case of the former, we have a silica-rich continental (land) volcano; in the latter, a low-silica oceanic volcano. Increased silica from continental rocks makes the Mt. St. Helens magma more viscous, less able to release pressure of contained gases, and therefore more subject to sudden bursts relieving this pressure. The magma of oceanic volcanoes, being more fluid, allows the gases to escape without pressure. Thus the Hawaiian volcanic magma flows like honey, while the Mt. St. Helens magma more often forms a bubble gum-like dome subject to sudden bursts.

Kinds of Volcanoes

As previously indicated, volcanoes vary depending on the composition of the molten rock material and the processes by which they are ejected at the Earth's surface. Two of the more familiar types of volcanoes are *shield volcanoes* (as in Hawaii), formed by fluid basaltic (low silica) lava, and *composit volcanoes* (as in the Cascade Mountain Range), formed by more viscous lava of andesite or dacite rock composition. Hawaiian volcanoes are fairly simple, being formed when the low viscosity lava flows out, forming squat, wide hills resembling a knight's shield. The composit volcano forms a steeper, conical hill by a variety of eruptive processes: blasts of debris (called tephra) that include everything from large blocks to fine ash; hot avalanches (pyroclastic flows); bulbous extrusions of sticky, viscous magma (called domes); and lava flows.

Mt. St. Helens is a composit volcano which contains deposits of many types just listed. It owes much of its conical form to debris from domes at its summit and flanks pushed out during previous eruptions.

How Does A Volcano Erupt?

The eruption of Mt. St. Helens can be explained as four development stages, though not every stage is clearly separated from the others.

Stage 1 — Earthquakes

When shocks are generated by movement of magma at great depths, earthquakes of the first stage may be generated without any disturbance at the surface of the earth.

Stage 2 — Phreatic Eruptions

Eruptions by steam blasts (phreatic eruptions) may occur when heat from the molten magma comes into contact with ground water contained within openings in rocks near the Earth's surface. Fragments of rocks (breccia) may be ground up and ejected with the steam, but newly solidified molten magma is not present.

Stage 3 — Magmatic Eruptions

Powerful eruptions of newly solidified magma fragments and gases may burst through to the surface when gas and fluid pressures in the magma overcome the confining pressure of the overlying rocks. The force may be explosive due to "boiling" of the molten rock when confining pressure is eliminated.

Stage 4 — Surface Magma

Molten magma may eventually rise to the surface of the earth, extruding to form flows, pools, or domes in the crater or on the flanks of a volcano.

At this writing Mt. St. Helens has progressed through all four stages with Stage 4 appearing in the form of a lava dome. The lava dome, shaped like a mushroom, was first sighted June 14th, growing by June 18th to an approximate size of 280 feet high by 660 feet in diameter. As the lava contained in this dome is stiff and viscous, there is little chance that it will flow down the mountain. Instead it will likely explode proving extremely dangerous to anyone in the immediate area. It is difficult to predict when the explosions will occur. Auxiliary domes may form around the initial dome before any explosion takes place. Or once the present dome explodes, auxiliary domes may form in its place. Whether it completes Stage 4 at this time, or not, it is in no hurry. In its own good, geological time, Mt. St. Helens will probably erupt again and again, slowly building one more portion of the land we live on.

STAGE 1 3.

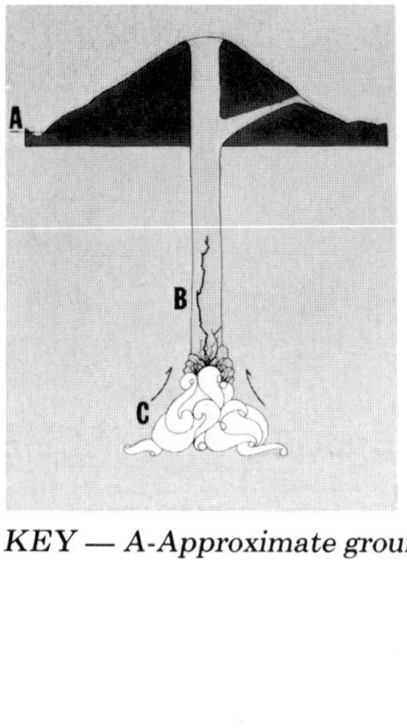

STAGE 2 4.

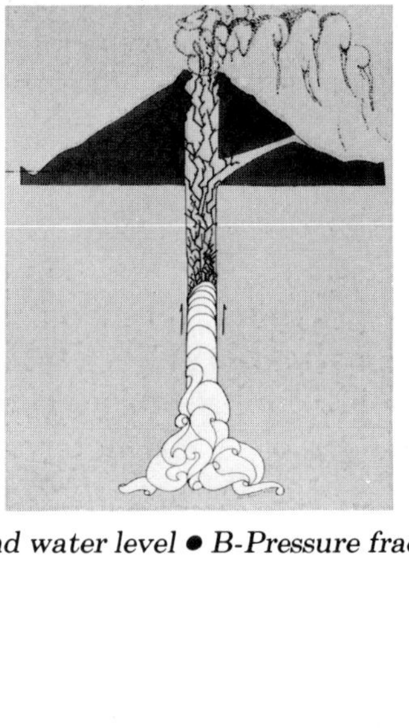

STAGE 3 5.

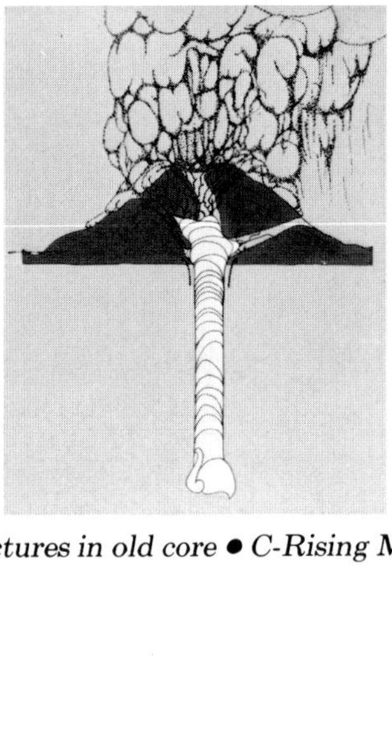

STAGE 4 6.

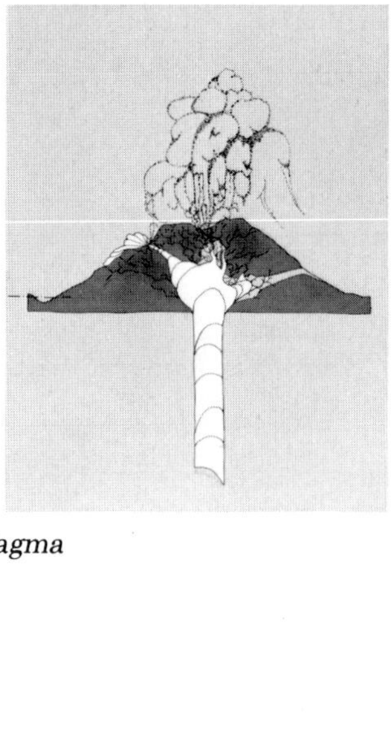

KEY — A-Approximate ground water level ● B-Pressure fractures in old core ● C-Rising Magma

FD
US 123

2

NATURE, GRIM AND DRAMATIC: A GEOLOGIST'S JOURNAL OF THE ERUPTION

Prof. Leonard Palmer, Portland State University

Tragedy At Coldwater One

The piece of 35-millimeter film in my hands was unlike any I had ever seen. It had no image on it and the emulsion had been burned so that only small patches of what was originally there still remained. I could see the sprocket holes and the shape of the film, but it was now curled and warped. The photographer using it had been seven miles away from Mt. St. Helens when the volcano erupted.

The film belonged to photographer, Reid Blackburn, who had most probably triggered the automatic cameras and was taking pictures with this equipment at the time Mt. St. Helens exploded, about 8:30 AM on May 18, 1980. The day after the blast a young helicopter pilot named Chris Lane flew a colleague and myself up to where Blackburn had been, the campsite called Coldwater One, where the cameras were being radio controlled. As we drew closer I experienced the kind of feeling that I don't think I'll ever forget. But there was too much of an overload of emotions to be able to put words around it then.

We could see the top of a Volvo sedan sitting above the ash. The ash deposits around it on the road were about even with the trunk lid and the engine hood. As we flew by we could see no sign at all of disturbance of the ash. We circled again to come closer to make sure that there was no one in the car; possibly Reid was waiting inside for someone to rescue him. But as we came nearer we could see that the win-

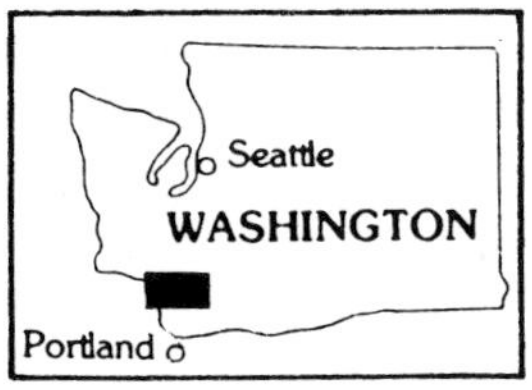

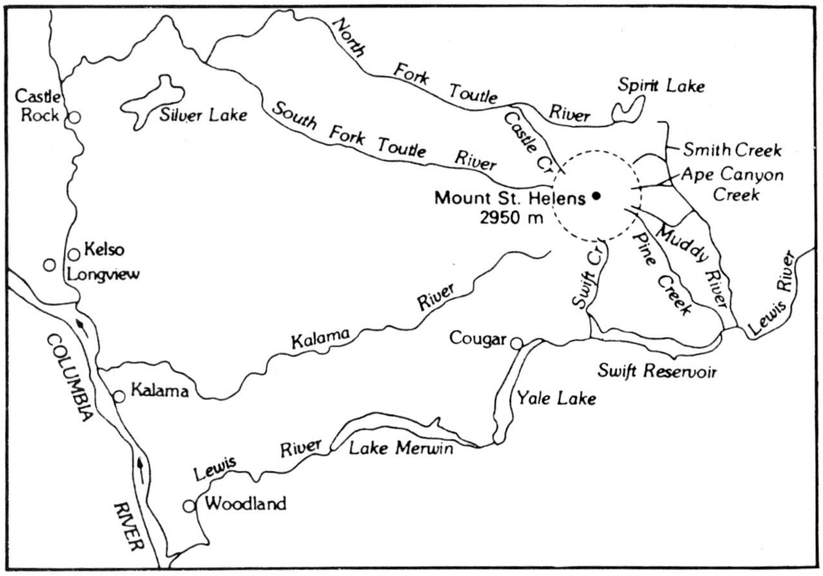

7. PHOTO LEFT: The once majestic beauty of Mt. St. Helens.

8. Map of Mt. St. Helens' region. Base of volcano shown as a dotted circle.

dows were shattered in the front and blasted completely out in the back and on the side facing the mountain. The inside of the car was full of dust, so that the seats were covered up to window level. There was no sign of Blackburn in the car.

I now know that he was in that car. I can't know for certain what happened to him on that morning. I'm aware that Reid Blackburn was a very capable young man. He was likely witnessing the eruption of Mt. St. Helens, saw the blast come toward him at a tremendous rate of speed and had time to respond, rushing into his car as a possible form of protection against the blast as it approached. Unfortunately that was futile because the blast destroyed the windows and the dust was so powerful that it was suffocating. The heat of the blast at that point would also have been extremely uncomfortable and I think he very quickly lost not only the air to breathe, but also the ability to breathe. And died, mercifully, within seconds.

There are such terrible ironies here. Mt. St. Helens, with its symmetrical cone, was one of the most beautiful mountains in the Northwest — it has been called the Fujiyama of America. But Mt. St. Helens is also the most active volcano in the Cascade Range. The eruption which started out with such killing blast force later developed a tremendous vertical thrust with material rising probably greater than the speed of sound, 65,000 feet into the sky with a hot plume recorded on infrared radar that measured the heat at an incandescent 400 degrees Celsius.

The ash from the eruption was so thick downwind toward Yakima and Spokane that the day was turned into night in some places. Where there was not chaos, there was confusion. And, very remindful of the Biblical stories we all grew up with, there was much death and destruction upon the land.

Most of the northwestern section of this country west of Idaho had been formed through volcanic processes. Nature destroys, nature rebuilds, nature destroys again. There is no fixed, predictable pattern. And the savage scar left by the latest volcanic activity of Mt. St. Helens on the lovely forests, lakes and countryside was evidence, grim and dramatic, that the process goes on as it has always done. The earth vibrates to its own rhythms.

How It All Started

The first evidence of possible renewed activity at Mt. St. Helens was on Thursday, March 27, 1980. When I stopped by Portland State University's Earth Sciences Department during the Spring break, there was an earthquake on our seismic recorder recognizable as a fairly local quake by its high frequency — as opposed to the slow rumble of distant quakes — and its characteristic vibration pattern. Information from other seismic stations confirmed that the earthquake had occurred somewhere in the vicinity of Longview, Washington — interesting, but nothing to cause concern. However, small, local quakes were occurring on Saturday, and

9. & 10. Scientists and geologists set up monitoring stations to measure and watch progress of volcanic activity.

SEISMOGRAPH READINGS SHOW VIBRATIONS FROM WITHIN THE VOLCANO.

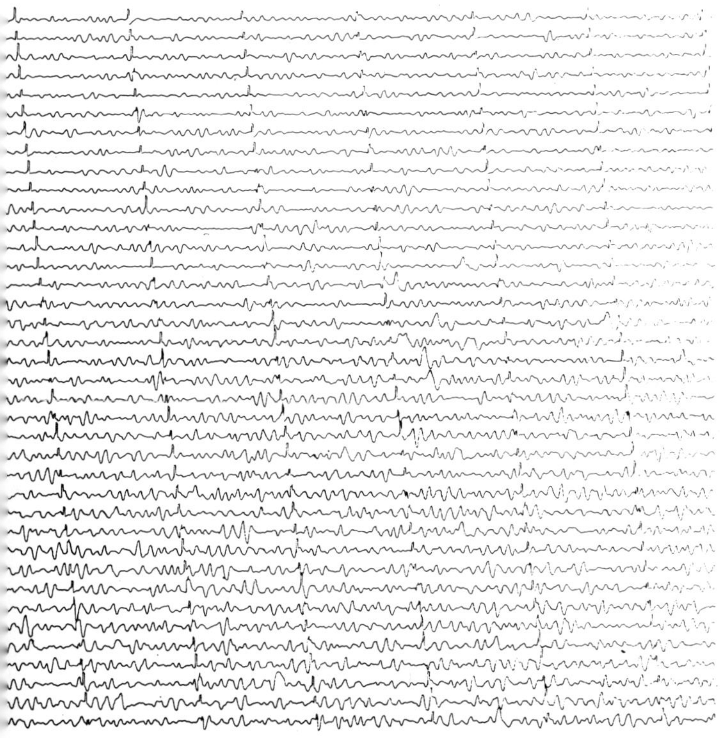

March 17th – Relatively Inactive.

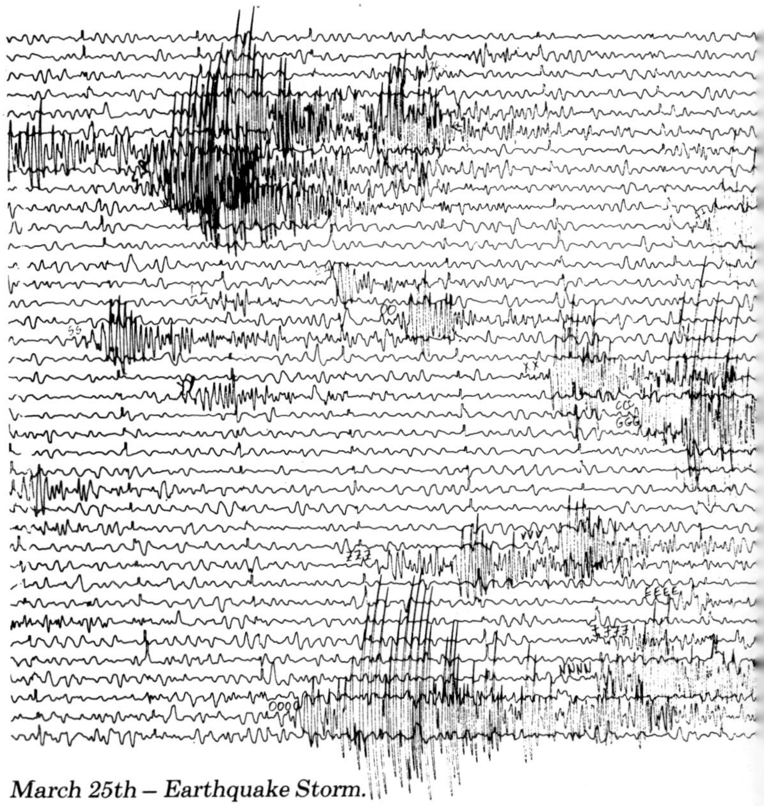

March 25th – Earthquake Storm.

again on Sunday, that were found to *originate* at Mt. St. Helens. The quakes increased in number on Monday and an earthquake "storm" occurred on the fourth day, Tuesday, March 25th.

This was really exciting! We had never seen so many local earthquakes before. The local press was invited in by the University's public relations people to look at our seismic records and to talk with geologists in the department, including Paul Hammond, our volcanologist and Ansel Johnson, our seismologist. I also spoke with the press. The following day headlines in the local newspaper quoted an expert who predicted that an eruption was imminent and that the volcano could "blow in days." To my considerable surprise, *I* was that "expert." And the reader had to plow deep into the story to find the caution that the volcano could also subside and do nothing.

The quote was picked up by the wire services and spread across the country and I began to hope that the mountain would erupt for reasons other than my geological curiosity. My colleagues at other universities considered the prediction somewhat rash and inflammatory and they were probably right. But two days later on Thursday, March 27th, one week after the first seismic earthquake occurred, there was a small volcanic event to save me from embarrassment.

Invited to have a look at the eruption with the KOIN-TV news team, we arrived via helicopter at the volcano at four o'clock in the afternoon, not long after the eruption had occurred. We found that a small, football-shaped crater (about thirty feet by ninety feet in size) had developed in the northern side of the old summit area between the snow pack and the cinders of the old crater wall. A very interesting fracture pattern was immediately apparent, extending all the way around the inner crest of the crater and down toward the north flanks of the mountain. And a small peak of snow on the north rim of the mountain was thrust up about thirty feet. Small craters, one

13. Small crater develops along with uplift of a thirty-foot peak.

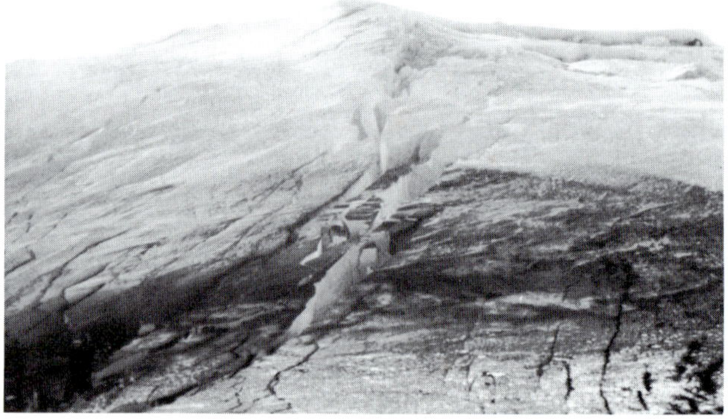

14. Fractures appear on the summit area.

15. Steam blasts emit ice and snow from small crater, scattering ash on the summit.

to two feet in diameter marked the fall of small blocks of ice or rock thrown out by the blast. This first small steam blast was accompanied by a decided drop in elevation of the summit area along east-west faults, and by northward bulging of the upper north flank of the peak as shown by criss-crossed fracturing of the mountain surface. It was clear that more than just steam was pushing from below.

16.

16. Small depressions in the snow show evidence of multiple eruptions.

17. ABOVE: Gravity-flow cloud of ash-laden vapor dropping particles onto the mountain surface and billowing back into the sky.

18. BELOW: March 30th Sunset over Mt. St. Helens.

19. Dark ash deposits absorb heat causing avalanches and ice flows.

After this information was rushed back to the studio for the evening news, we immediately returned to the mountain and could see that the summit fractures had almost doubled in size. Small steam puffs floated out from the crater and we were all ecstatic. We had an active volcano!

Within hours, teams of media people and geologists were congregating to see what was happening. But cloudy weather closed in so that all we saw on Friday and Saturday were puffs of steam billowing through the clouds and drifting downwind, forming a cloud shaped like a fence made of cotton. We could see very little of what was happening to the mountain.

Our next chance for a clear look was on Sunday morning, March 30th, four days after the original eruption. During the night the United States Geological Survey (USGS) had reported a glow visible in the crater with an arc flashing, like gas or lightning, of "sharp blue color." The day dawned clear and sunny and when we flew up at nine o'clock in the morning, the mountain was a spectacular sight — the western half of the cone was white with new snow, while the eastern half was covered with dark ash. An eruption was just finishing and a dark brown cloud flowed over the north rim of the crater, swept down the south flank of the mountain and appeared to be dropping ash onto the slope. Downwind, a high, fuzzy dark cloud of ash drifted southeastward at about 15,000 altitude. Joe Stein at the small community of Zig Zag near Mt. Hood later told me that he came out of church to find his automobile dusted with ash; but no great nuisance was caused there, or to the Portland water supply reservoir nearby at Bull Run.

This was a time of high spirits — these early eruptions brought cheers from pilots and reporters who happened to be flying near the mountain whenever an eruption occurred. They should also have cheered not bumping into each other in this great traffic jam in the sky. Radar documented over 250 aircraft in the Mt. St. Helens' area that Sunday. Air traffic was controlled within a ten-mile radius by allowing only one plane at each 500-foot vertical interval, all circling counterclockwise. As a result, most aircraft had to circle along at the ten-mile boundary for an hour or two before getting their chance for a closer look, but a few eager-beavers risked collision by flying into the restricted area illegally.

By now we could see that the summit had developed a second crater. The first crater had expanded into a circle 200 feet in diameter, and a new larger crater about 500 feet in diameter had formed toward the southwest side of the summit. The walls of these craters now exposed about fifty to seventy-five feet of snow pack and ice over rocks. The summit area had dropped down about fifty feet along fractures which now extended almost east-west across the summit, but angled northward as they extended down the flanks of the mountain.

The clear weather of early April warmed the

dark ash-covered snow on the mountain slopes. Since the predominant winds had carried most deposits eastward, that side of the mountain had experienced flows of dark material which swept out across the plains at the base of the mountain. First reports called these "mudflows," but my colleague, Marvin Beeson, was able to fly low with a news team and saw that 95 percent of the flows were ice material, and should more appropriately be called "ice-flows." These had been caused by ice avalanches high on the mountain. Their path down the mountain resembled a toboggan run. Small mudflows had formed on the mountain's flanks, but most were not as large as the ice-flows.

From the 31st of March until the 12th of April the steam eruptions continued to expand the existing crater areas while the summit continued to drop downward and the north flank bulged northward. Only the south side of the mountain appeared to be stable. Fresh snow and ash deposits were repeatedly broken by the fracture movements. The northward sliding of the "bulge," as it came to be called, widened the crest of the volcano.

As early as April 2nd, the fault-steepened south wall of the now-combined craters had developed caving and sliding that formed a ragged third cavity. This extended from the first two to form a very crude three-leaf clover pattern. Continuation of these processes throughout April resulted in the creation of a pear-shaped crater about 1000 by 1500 feet, slightly smaller to the east and steeper on the south side. At its maximum depth, it measured at least 700 to 800 feet from the south summit to the bottom, about twice the height of a

20. Terminal end of ice flows.

21. Formation of two craters after initial eruption.

22. Clover-leaf pattern formed as a result of craters joining.

23. Crater deepens as faults continue to break the surface.

24. By late April a pear-shaped crater formed.

forty-storied building. The area could contain twenty-four football fields.

Frequent eruptive venting continued to be observed through April whenever the weather was favorable for viewing. Many spectacular shapes of weather and eruptive clouds were photographed including (1) white vapor, (2) brown eruptive clouds (apparently containing much heavy ash reducing their bouyancy), and (3) jets of black rock fragments. All combinations of these were seen, and at times a white shield-shaped cloud capped the entire mountain.

A large eruption might rise over a mile above the crater (over 14,000 feet in elevation), a moderate-sized eruption 1000 feet above, and a small eruption only a hundred feet or so. The recurrence of eruptions was of course not predictable. However, even on flights without an eruption, observations of the changing crater shape needed to be recorded. But any proper volcano ought to show some "smoke" — after all, most picture books of volcanoes concentrate on the spectacular eruptive plumes.

On an April 10th flight at 10:00 AM, we were particularly lucky in seeing an example of the progressive development of an eruption with most of the normal types of eruptive plumes. It began as a small white puff of vapor as we approached the mountain. It grew during a period of three to five minutes into a white plume rising to 1,000 feet above the summit. As we circled upwind above the crater and

ASH ERUPTION, APRIL 13th, DIFFERENT VIEWS FROM THE GROUND.

25.

26.

27.

28.

29.

AERIAL VIEWS OF MT. ST. HELENS PRIOR TO THE MAY 18TH ERUPTION.

30.

31.

32.

33.

34.

35. PHOTO RIGHT: Vapor eruption caused by Mt. St. Helens own thermal content rather than entirely from eruptive forces.

50. A view towards the west shows a thick snow cover; rocks thrown out of the crater by eruptions litter the surface.

51. The faulting of the south summit area has caused a steep, precipitous slope on the south side of the crater.

52. The scale of the crater may be appreciated by recognizing the size of the people working on the crater rim area. Ash accumulated on the west saddle rim to a depth of over twenty-five feet.

53. The protrusion upward of the north peak fractured rock material and snow.

54. Rocks ranging in size from a few feet to the length of an entire automobile crashed to the bottom of the crater to be blasted out later by future eruptions.

55. *Looking east a small steam fumarole vented white plumes constantly during the quiescent period of no eruptions.*

56. *Looking toward Mt. Adams, the precipitousness of the south wall of the crater was extremely hazardous with large rocks breaking loose during earthquake vibrations.*

57. *Overhanging blocks of snow on the south rim of the crater made viewing from this angle unwise without appropriate climbing ropes secured.*

scouted the edge of the crater for some vertical fracture from which I could collect. I was lucky to find the upper crater rim freshly exposed and unfrozen. It was easy to cut steps into the loose material and climb down the crater wall while filling sample bags. The fresh deposit over glacial ice was twenty-six-feet thick in layers ranging from one inch to about a foot. Each layer had coarser rock chips at the base grading upward into sandy grains. Later analysis would determine this material to be broken from rocks of the existing mountain, not from a magmatic eruption.

A number of other geological investigators had been to the top, but the news coverage given to my trip convinced the USGS to disassociate itself from my volcano work. So even though a second trip to the top with a larger university crew and a more discreet sponsor went smoothly a week later, the damage had been done. I was out of the remote camera project and my next clearance permit was shuffled for two weeks and finally lost in the bureaucracy. However, this time I could afford to be philosophical since I had been lucky to get in at all; most scientists were obstructed by the red tape unless they could get in with a news group.

Fortunately I was able to join ranks with KOIN-TV's news team and got back to the mountain. But both the weather and television budgets, strained by flight time expenses, were reducing the number of flights there. Meanwhile the earthquakes continued to decrease slightly in number per day, but the number of quakes over magnitude four increased. It was still very much a wait-and-see game.

Finally in late April the steam eruptions almost stopped after four weeks of activity. Whisps of steam continued from various vents, called fumaroles, in and adjacent to the crater. Mt. St. Helens had become calm. But as the old saying goes, it was merely the calm before the storm.

During the weeks preceding this period of deceptive calm, the authorities had taken great pains to insure public safety. Parts of the area near and adjacent to Mt. St. Helens were evacuated as precautionary measures. Spirit Lake, which lies directly below the danger area, was evacuated and most residents left very willingly, realizing the dangers. Others were not so willing. Eighty-four-year-old Harry Truman was one of those who were not

58. (ABOVE) and 59. (BELOW): Different views of the mountain.

60. *March 31st.*

61. *April 4th.*

62. *April 20th. .*

63. *May 11th.*

64. *May 16th.*

60.-64. Consecutive photographic documentation showing fracturing of the east side of the crater, the lowering of the saddle-horn-like feature to the north, and the progressive expansion of the bulge until it was a large dome protruding northward. All photos prior to a landslide causing its failure on May 18th.

65. March 30th.

66. April 10th.

67. April 30th.

68. May 11th.

69. May 16th.

65.-69. A profile of the bulge area on the north flank of the mountain shows a progressive breaking of formerly smooth surface and an uplifting of the entire flank of mountain above its former position until the whole mountain protruded northward very noticeably even from a distance.

WESTERN GRABEN, DOWN-DROP BLOCK AT SUMMIT.

70. March 30th — From the west a large block of the mountain was seen to drop downward and the north side of the mountain expanded out toward the north (left) in this view. Within the first few days extensive fractures extended down the west flank of the mountain showing the cracking apart of the original volcanic cone.

71. March 31st — Fresh snowfall obscured old fractures but significant displacements along the fault of the old summit showed continuing dropping of the crater area.

72. April 2nd — Fresh breaking of the faults on the south side of the summit extended well over 1,000 feet down and sloping toward the north.

73. April 4th — New ash continually changed the apppearance of the crater area.

74. April 30th — As the summit dropped to more than 200 feet, the bulge was at the same time pushing northward and had formed a second peak at the summit area extending about 100 feet upward and outward.

75. May 11th — A considerable offset had occurred between the apparently stable south flank of the mountain and the down-dropping and expanding block to the left.

76. May 16th — Just before the failure of the north side of the mountain by landslide, the highly fractured mass of material had offset what appeared to be 200-300 feet along the fault of the south side of the crater. Rock masses were beginning to fail and roll down the surface indicating the instability at this time.

77-81. These photos look south directly at the upper bulge area. The early fracturing pattern with remnants of the original mountain surface are clearly visible in March and early April. By mid-April and early May the surface was almost entirely fractured with faults resulting from the deformation of some type of pushing by the magma below.

77. March 21st.

78. April 2nd.

79. April 13th.

80. May 11th.

81. May 15th.

82. PHOTO LEFT: Close-up views of the center of the bulge area show the progressive reduction in size of blocks, fragments within that rock mass, until finally the fracture rubble was falling and working itself downhill. An entire second "saddlehorn" had formed where the bulge extended out from the mountain's original position.

82. April 2nd.

83. April 13th.

84. April 23rd.

85. May 4th.

86. May 16th.

so willing. Truman, operator of the St. Helens' Lodge, had spent most of his adult life on the mountain. During those evacuation days he made it perfectly clear to one and all that he did not intend to leave the mountain. His steadfast refusal to do so gave him the reputation of a stubborn, feisty, whiskey-drinking old diehard. School children wrote to Truman, asking him to leave the danger area. Sheriff's departments offered transportation. But all entreaties were refused. Harry Truman, crusty octogenarian, became, for a moment, a symbol of our confidence in the supremacy of man.

And Truman was not alone in his directional signals: there were others who went to Mt. St. Helens instead of leaving it. Through graduate students we learned of adventuresome climbers and photographers who slipped past the barricades or found roads without gates. In one instance I spent anxious hours helping a worried father search for his son, overdue from a climb. As it turned out, the young man, an inexperienced climber, had simply gotten lost. And when we finally made radio contact with him, he was appreciative of our concern but was also a little miffed — which gave his relieved father and me a good laugh.

One day at the summit a surprised government team arriving by helicopter was greeted by a bearded student, Robert Rogers, casually resting there on his sleeping bag. Rogers later photographed the initial eruption from a close vantage point. There were many like him — unrestrainable — but few so fortunate.

My own favorite moment of levity during this tense period concerned some ice used to make drinks. Ice from the glacier in the crater wall had been used by our team to keep frozen samples preserved on our way back to the university. That particular evening I shared the remainder of this ice with some of my university colleagues. Their drinks were cooler than some of their responses. Reactions ranged from *"Really? That's wonderful!"* to restrained terror *"How can you be sure it's safe?"*

There was also a moment that, upon reflection, makes me understandably proud of my profession. More than a week before the eruption on Sunday, May 18th, my good friend and colleague, Dr. Rick Kienle, told his client: "My simple calculations indicate a possible eruption on Friday." Kienle's familiarity with the Cascade volcanoes led him to stay away from the north side of Mt. St. Helens and to predict the uncorking of the mountain when the bulge expanded beyond the critical angle of repose. He reasoned that the removal of the weight of the bulge by landslides could trigger the eruption. And he was so right. Two days early, but so right.

87. Spirit Lake Lodge.

88. Harry Truman (third from Left).

89.

90.

91. Great volcanic activity as shown on seismograph reading from May 18th.

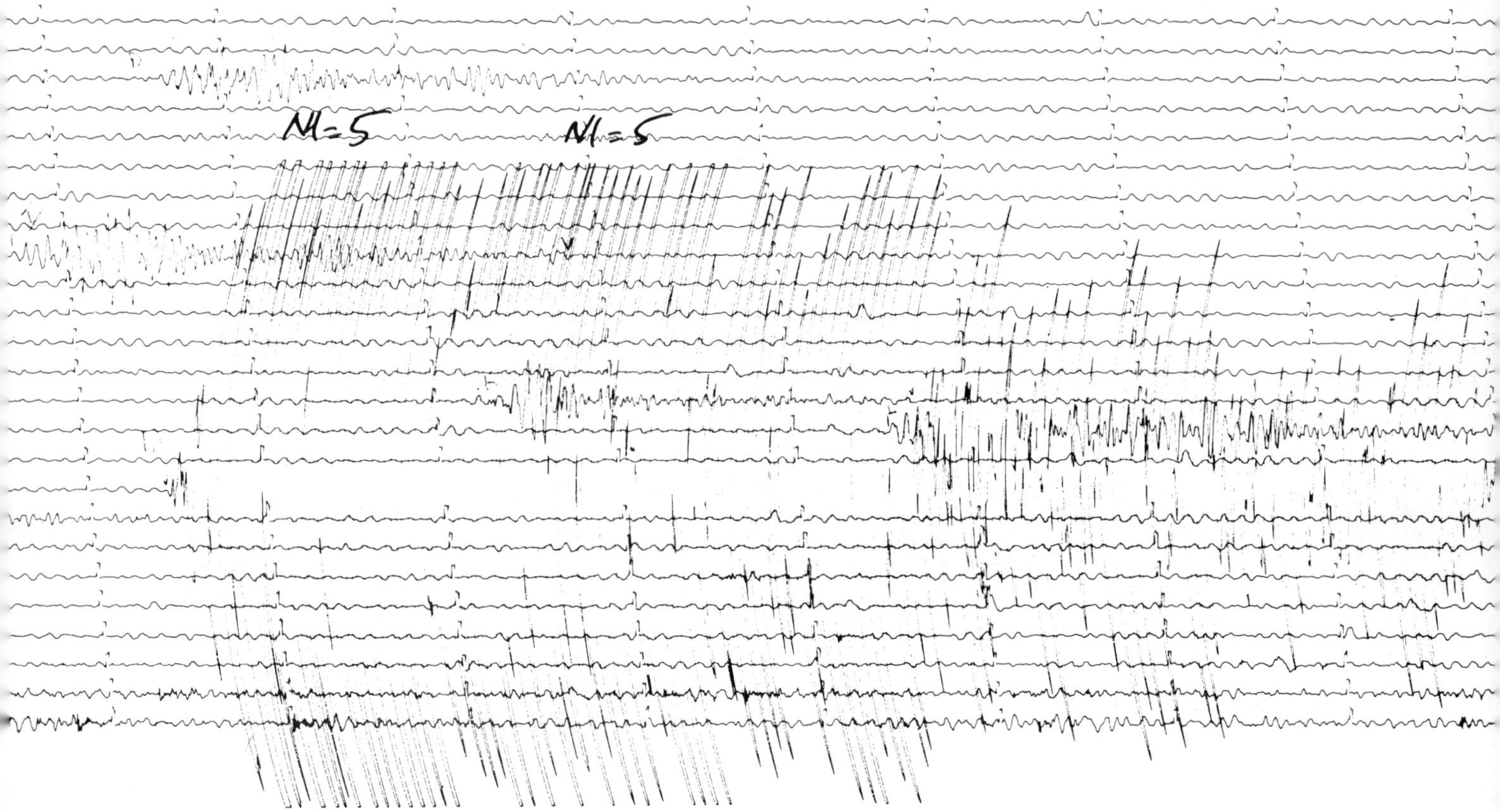

A phone call disrupted my tranquil Sunday morning puttering: "The mountain has erupted and radio communication is lost with Gerry Martin and Reid Blackburn on the north side." The emergency amateur radio network was once again the first with the information. One hundred and fifty miles east on a fossil-gathering trip, Dick Thoms was notified at the speed of sound by a sonic boom. (Yet I heard nothing in Portland.) Like Thoms, most of the other geology staff were out on field trips that weekend. By 10:00 AM I was in the air with KOIN-TV and the field trips were rapidly heading home.

92.-99. Photos beginning to the right: Gary Rosenquist was close enough to the mountain when it erupted to take the following shots and still live to talk about them. When looked at in sequence the photographs show exactly what happened that morning. These are the unique time-lapse photos that gained national attention. All photographs on pages 50-57 are © Gary Rosenquist/Earth Images

92. May 18th, Dawn.

93. May 18th, 8:00 AM PDT.

94. May 18th, 8:39:00 AM PDT (Approximate).

95. May 18th, 8:39:05 AM PDT (Approximate).

96. May 18th, 8:39:10 AM PDT (Approximate).

97. May 18th, 8:39:15 AM PDT (Approximate).

98. May 18th, 8:39:20 AM PDT (Approximate).

61.

02.

62.

63.

04.

64.

65.

3.

66.

108.-113. Weather Satellite Photos showing initial expansion and movement of ash cloud. On the first day alone the huge ash cloud spread eastward over eastern Washington, Idaho, and into Montana.

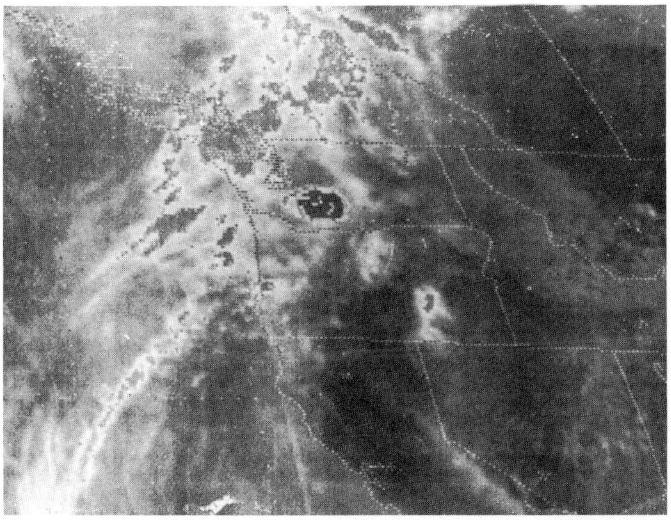

108. May 18th, 9:15 AM PDT.

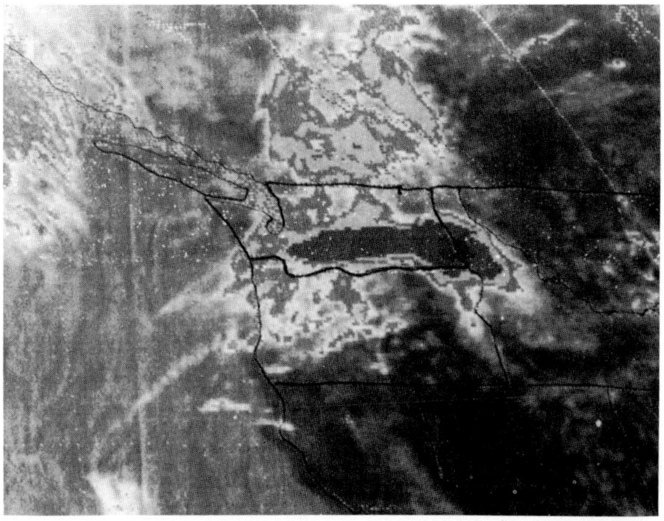

111. May 18th, 2:15 PM PDT.

109. May 18th, 10:15 AM PDT.

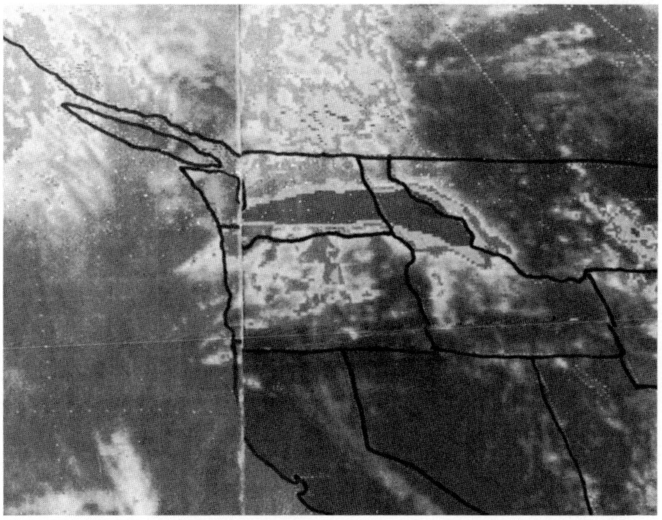

112. May 18th, 3:15 PM PDT.

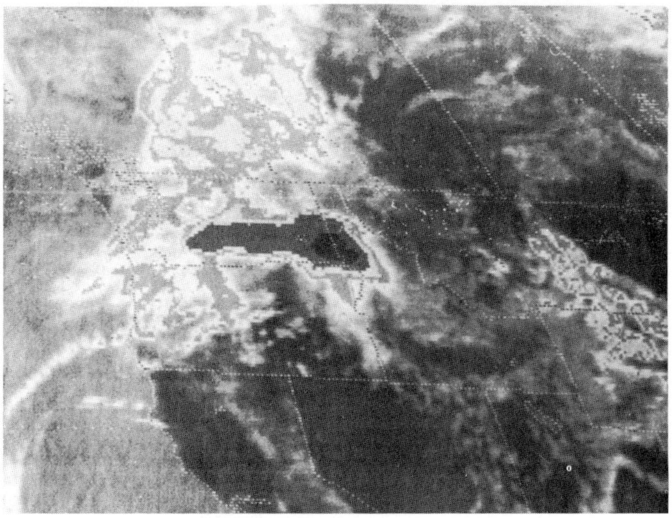

110. May 18th, 1:15 PM PDT.

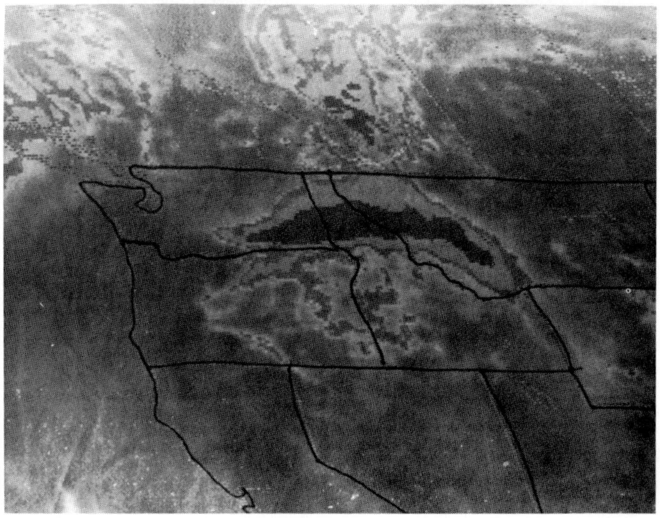

113. May 18th, 7:15 PM PDT.

114. Aerial view from 9,000 feet, May 18th, approximately 10:45 AM PDT.

Monday morning the Kelso airport was infested with helicopters. About fifteen military and at least half-a-dozen private helicopters spread along the taxiway. An Army Reserve pilot told me of mangled cars, deaths, blasted trees, dust, and debris. Full understanding of the event was getting increasingly difficult, yet at the same time, deeply sobering. I was feeling very distressed and wanted to go in for Gerry and Reid.

The Washington State National Guard was allowing the news media to accompany rescue missions in search of survivors. I joined those waiting their anxious turn at the rescue mission center at the Toutle High School athletic field. There was much coming and going: evacuees and worried property owners, photographers, reporters, and guardsmen billowing dust on their way to the Salvation Army refreshment trailer for a drink to wash their throats after a ground landing mission. Officers Dick Lattimer and Mark Kettelbrack were handling priorities in an effective and sympathetic way, but it seemed an eternity before an opportunity for my flight came up. By then my geology colleague, Marvin Beeson, had just arrived with a news crew from another TV station and I was able to include him in the mission.

The destination was Coldwater One, where Reid Blackburn had been, and the ridge to the northeast, where Gerry Martin had been.

115. PHOTO RIGHT: May 18th: A log jam combined with mud material begins its destructive march down the south fork of the Toutle River. Note still clear water which precedes the leading edge of the log jam.

116.-118. As river constricts at various points, the logs crash into each other, building an immense, advancing, destructive wall of debris.

116.

117.

119.-122. Since the mixture of mud and logs was much heavier than a normal flood, it flowed like concrete in a chute, crushing everything in its inexorable progress.

119.

121.

120.

122.

123. By early Sunday afternoon the north fork of the Toutle River was also clogged by a log jam.
The bridge above was one of the casualties.

124.-125. Mud overflows branches of the Toutle River. Pictured above are houses covered to their rooftops. Below is a view of the highway parallel to the River made impassable by the rampaging mud.

124.

125.

126.-127. More distant views showing damage inflicted by the now out-of-control mudflows.

126.

127.

128. Trucks swamped by overflow from the River.

129. A thick, white, fog-like cloud of ash obstructs view and makes rescue helicopter flights unsafe.

130. Bridge span lies tangled like a child's toy.

131. A path through the young timber more than 15 miles from the blast site looks as if a "hundred diameter finger had playfully swept across the forest."

132.-135. What had been pristine beauty only hours before now lay in total devastation.

132.

133.

134.

135.

136.-139. Blocks of ice could be found littered as far as eight miles from the mountain.

136.

137.

138.

139.

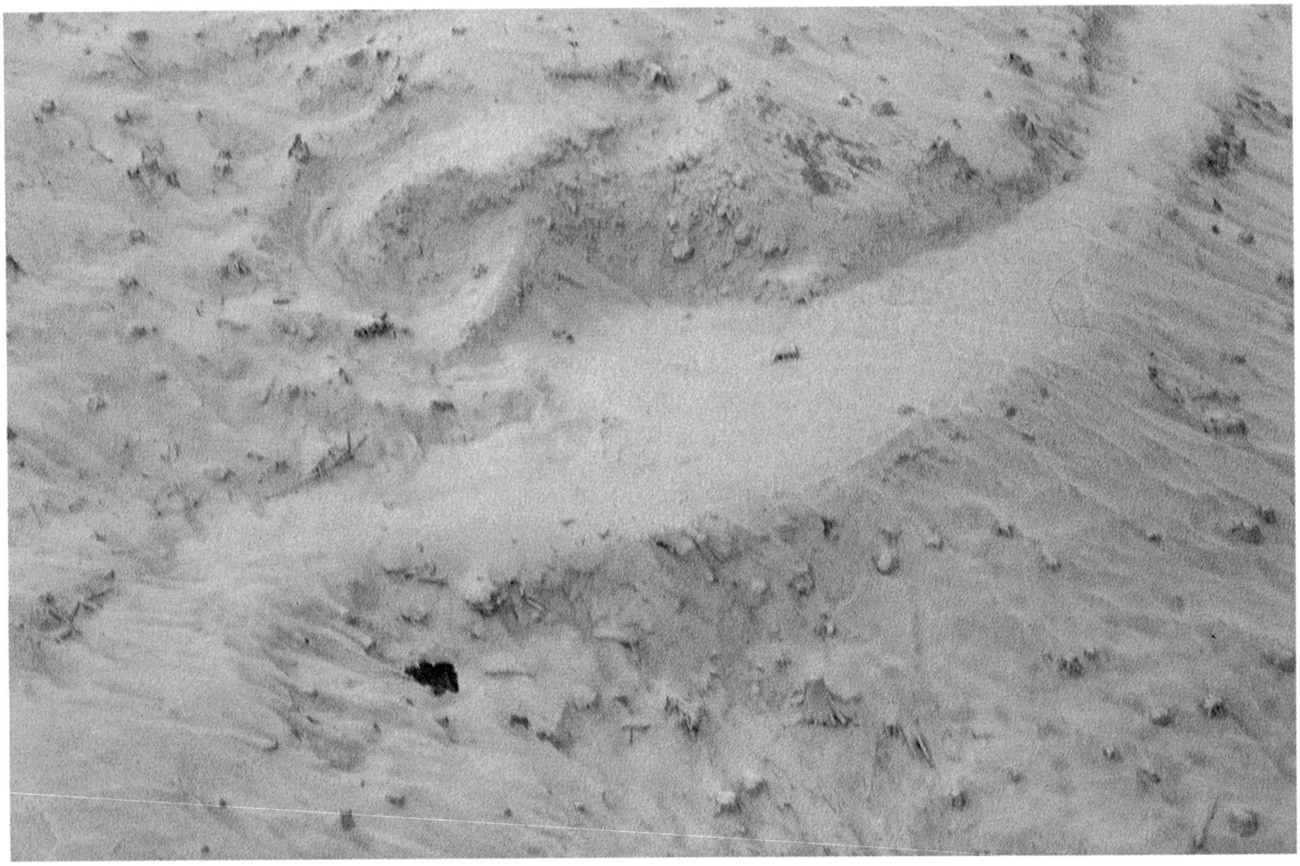

140. A thick shield of ash covers everything in the vicinity of the mountain.

Dwight Reber's earlier rescue trips to Coldwater One found dangerous conditions that made landing out of the question. The report he gave was equally bleak. No word had come from Gerry. There had been no reported sight of his motor home, but there were reports of radio clicking signals, like a microphone switched on without a voice.

As we flew up the wide mud swath of the North fork of the Toutle River with Chris Lane, we saw the destruction caused by the hot mudflows, or lahars. Houses were destroyed; open-top railroad cars floated off their tracks; even a bridge span tangled in mud. But nothing, not words nor geology textbooks, had prepared us for the sights to come.

First it was dust. The green land lost its color about twenty miles out from the volcano. Grey dust was plastered against the rock and on trees. On roadways and logging trails we could see tracks of deer and men, as if in fresh snow. Extending fifteen miles from the mountain, the valley floor was buried by a giant-sized mud pudding. Roads vanished under the goo. The flow appeared to be about ten to twenty feet thick with a top of greyish brown and large greyish white blotches fifty to one hundred feet across.

Another few miles up the valley the flow thickened into a pitted mass over one hundred feet thick. It is really impossible to describe. I have seen nothing like it — a very, very thick mass of ash, cinder, rock, ice, and other debris with pits and linear wedge-shaped depressions about one hundred feet deep in which a ten-storied building could stand without reaching above the surface. There were great, chaotic heaps of logs still burning, blocks of ice melting, and steam venting from the obviously hot debris.

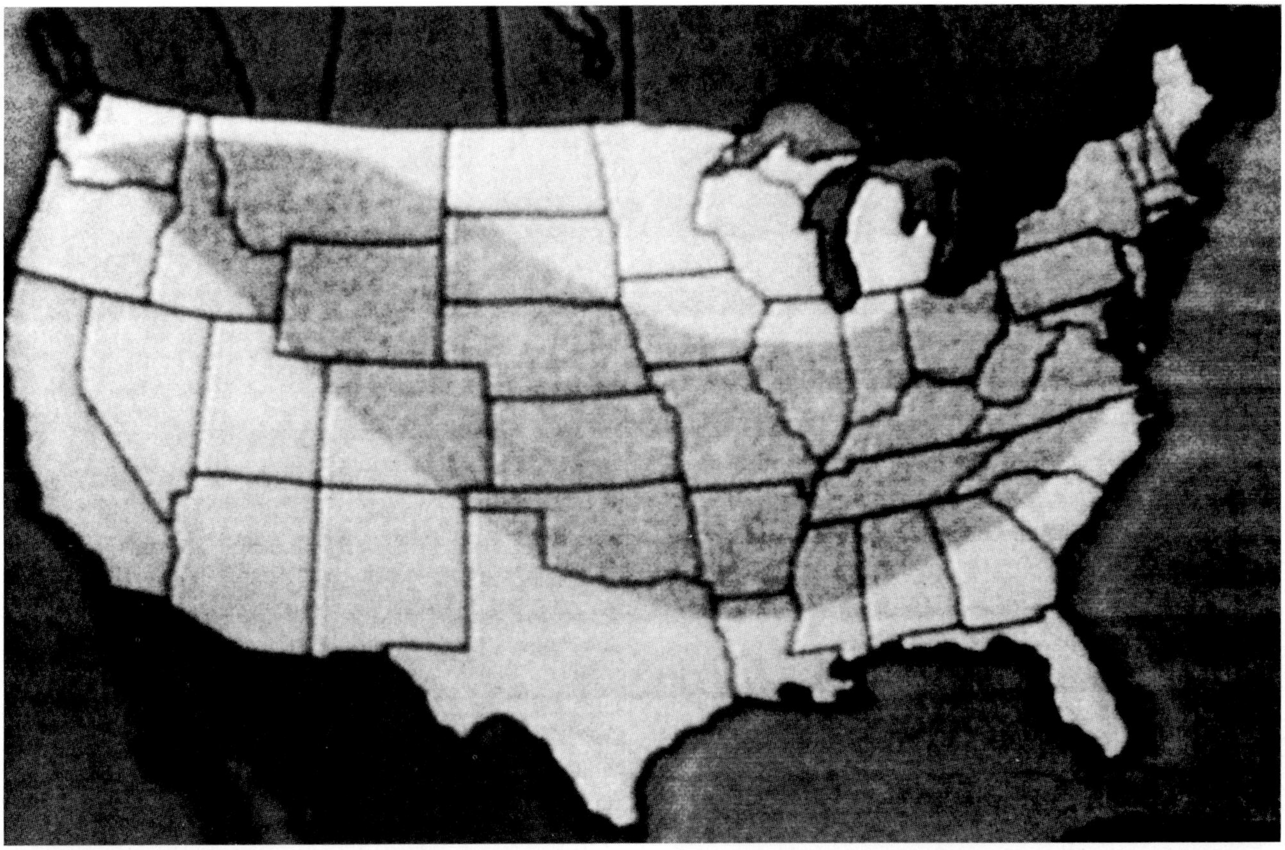

141. The May 18th eruption of Mt. St. Helens sent up an ash cloud so dense it blotted out the sun. Climbing to 60,000 feet, the cloud reached the jet stream and was carried across the country . . . eventually around the world.

142. 70X magnification of ash sample.

143. 280X magnification of ash sample.

144. 1400X magnification of ash sample.

145. 1400X magnification of ash sample.

146. Washington, where the ash fell heaviest: snorkle devices designed to prevent ash contamination were attached to local police cars.

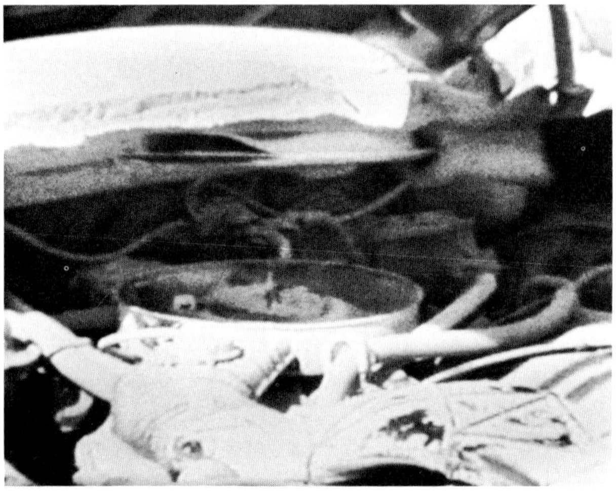

147. Cars came to a stop as carburetors choked on the ash-dust causing many motorists to be stranded.

148. People attacked ash with shovels and hose, scooping it up in large trucks and hauling it away.

149. Dark masses of wet ash ran down the slopes of the mountain across the lighter, dry ash material.

On the hillslopes the trees were first seen knocked down in swatches — as if torn out of the earth by the stroke of a 100-foot-diameter finger. Then, closer to the campsite, all of the trees had been blown down away from the mountain, lying in pathetic jumbles, deathly in their grey mantle of ash. About seven miles from the mountain, the trees lay exactly aligned parallel to one another, their roots toward the blast and their limbs stripped away entirely. A fog-like white cloud of ash and vapor obscured the Spirit Lake area to the east, fuming steam vented from craters on the valley floor, fires burned here and there in the trees. It was prehistoric, a hell-like place. This was Coldwater One.

Reid Blackburn's Volvo sat buried deep in ash. None of the rest of the camp was visible. I had maintained the hope that he might have been able to find protection in the car and we were anxious to land as close by as possible. But, as we flew in, I could see the windows toward the mountain broken and blown out and the car full of ash. No one could be alive in that car. Clouds of ash billowed into the air after our low pass, making landing extremely dangerous with no visibility in the stirred-up dust. Similarly, only a brief pass could be made

150. The crest of the mountain was lowered to just over 8,000 feet by the May 18th eruption.
Hot vapors rise from the newly-formed crater area.

151. Closer view of the crater area. While hot and fuming jets of magmatic material rise from the center of the crater, still hot residue of blasted material fills the bottom of the valley.

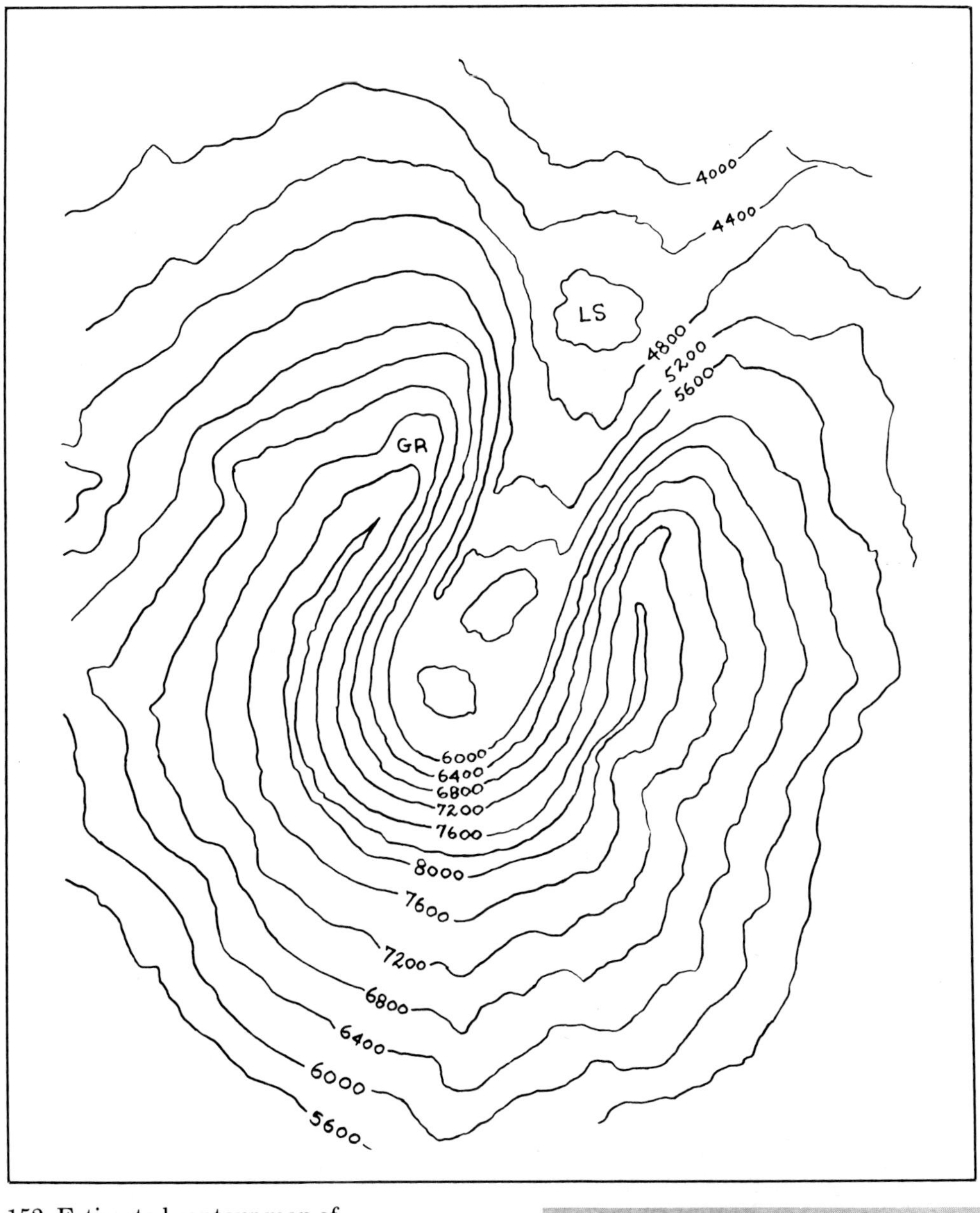

152. Estimated contour map of new crater by Dr. John Allen, Portland State University geologist. Copied with permission.

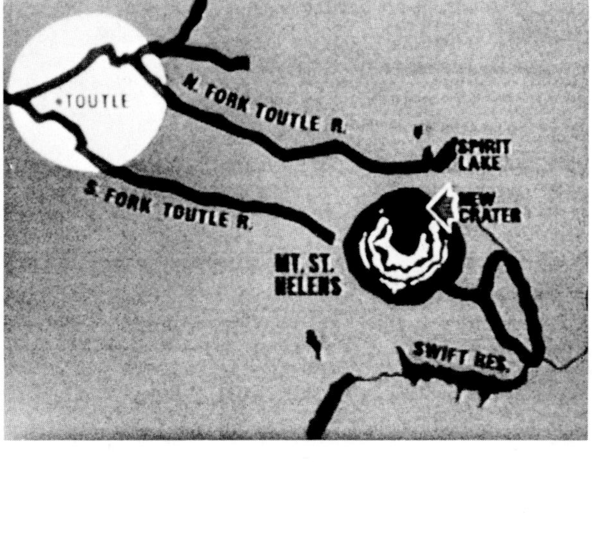

153. Illustration showing relationship of Mt. St. Helens to the town of Toutle.

along the ridge where Gerry Martin had been reported. Other rescue flights were active in that area and visibility was poor. I did observe that the motor home was gone. I would have preferred to stay and keep searching, but now the radio was calling us to another rescue mission east of Mt. St. Helens.

This time our mission was to look for a family at Sunrise Peak, seventeen miles east of the mountain. We flew south around the mountain to avoid the ash plume. The eruption was waning to a plume a few hundred feet high and the top of the mountain was gone, lowered by a thousand feet or more. An Air Force rescue helicopter out from Portland joined our mission, their crew highly skilled and with long experience in this area — it seemed as though they knew every hill for miles around from past climbing and camping experience.

As we passed Cinnamon Peak, the site of our original planned remote control station, the land was still green and ash free. A pity the site was moved — the change had likely cost Reid Blackburn his life.

Flying southeast of the mountain, mudflows were apparent on the Muddy River and Pine Creek, but the headwaters were obscured by the clouds. Pyroclastic blasts down these streams that flow into Swift Reservoir represented a serious threat to the safety of the dams and could result in potential floods downstream. I made a note to verify that the managers of the reservoir were informed on the upstream conditions and were aware of the conditions of the blast on the opposite side. I wasn't confident that anyone could really explain what I had just seen.

The search mission was thorough but unsuccessful. We found deer tracks, but no human signs of life; apparently there had been an error in location or else a false report. Keeping track of the other helicopter was difficult in the poor visibility and I was glad to be of some use in navigating, using my flying skills and local familiarity with the area. It was a diversion from the traumatizing effects of what we had seen.

Marvin Beeson and I were quite late getting home that night. We were bone-weary and very somber. It had been a day of wonder and awe; a day of deep grief and pain; a private day of introspection and appreciation for the natural laws fundamental to my profession over which man never had, nor ever will, exert any control. Mt. St. Helens was awake again and we must live with the consequences.

154.-155. The center of the newly-created crater walls are extremely steep inside. A very large portion of the former conical peak was entirely blasted away to the valley below and through the air, propelled to places toward the northwest.

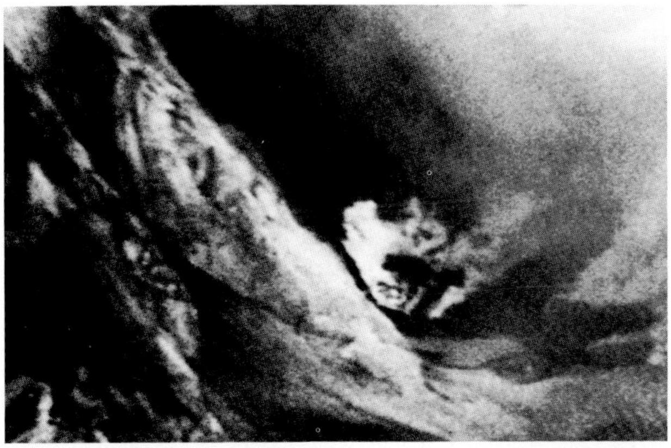

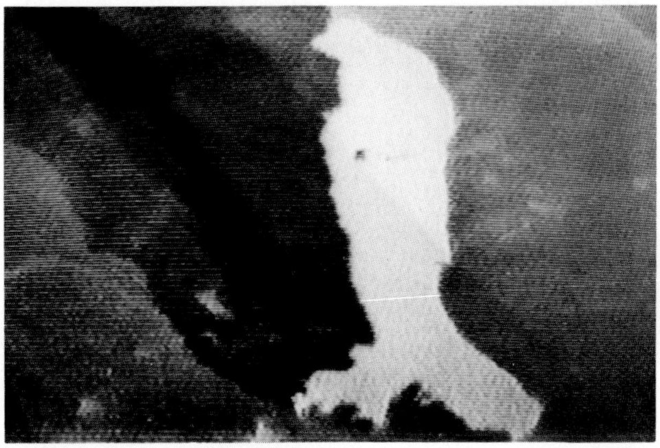

156.-159. Upper left is a picture of the crater area as the human eye sees it.
To the right of it is an infrared picture of the same crater.
In the infrared shot what appears as white is very hot,
with the black areas being the cooler portions. Infrared pictures are
images taken not with any light, but only with heat.
Infrared shot shows temperatures rising above 400 degrees in
the crater area and on the floor of the canyon coming
out of the crater. The second set is a picture of
Spirit Lake (to the left) and an infrared image,
taken on May 31st, of the same area.

90.

160.

161.

160.-172. Photos beginning on page 90: On June 4th the Newsroom 6 helicopter covered
the grim task of removing the twenty-fourth victim from the blast zone.
Pictures beginning on the facing page and continuing
over the next six pages show the utter desolation left by the May 18th eruption
as viewed by crew members taking part in the recovery mission.

162.

166.

163.

167.

164.

168.

165.

169.

170.

94.

95.

72.

173.

3

PREDICTIONS AND AFTERMATH

As the entire world knows, Mt. St. Helens erupted on May 18, 1980. And again a week later. And again the second week in June. When would it end? Or would it end? No one, not even the most brilliant of the earth scientists, could predict the now-and-future activity of the once-majestic mountain with certainty. Earth does not give up its secrets that easily . . . if at all.

If Mt. St. Helens had been quiet in this century, it was certainly not the case during the century previous. We know of the considerable violent activity of the volcano then, from an interesting melange of sources. These include Indian legends and myths, as well as eye witness accounts of the eruption of 1800, later shared with white settlers. There were also missionaries, settlers and explorers, plus an occasional intrepid wandering journalist, who witnessed the eruptions of 1831 and 1835 and the intermittent 1842-57 "Great Eruption" period. And then of course we have had extensive geological study of the volcano and surrounding area which has determined that the previous, most explosive, activity of Mt. St. Helens was several hundred years ago, roughly around the time that Columbus landed in America. We know that very large quantities of pumice and fine ash were blasted into the air and settled over a wide area. This was the most violent eruption in Mt. St. Helens' history over a 3,000-year period prior to the events of May 18.

It is also fascinating to compare the various accounts of eruptions during the past century with our scientific knowledge of the events. The reports of "beautiful scrolls of what seemed to be pure steam," "vast columns of lurid smoke and fire," considerable periods of "dense darkness" and waves of lava or mud-

TABLE — Eruptions and dormant intervals at Mount St. Helens since 2500 B.C. (Crandell and others, 1975)

(The circles represent specific eruptions that were observed or that have been dated or closely bracketed by radiocarbon age determinations; the vertical boxes represent dormant intervals)

A.D. 1900	Dormant interval of 120 years
	Dome and tephra eruptions, lava flows (?)
1800	Tephra eruption, mudflows
	Apparent dormant interval of ca. 150 years
1700	
	Pyroclastic flows Dome eruption, mudflows
1600	
	Apparent dormant interval of ca. 100 years
1500	Tephra eruptions, pyroclastic flows
1400	Pyroclastic flows
SCALE CHANGE 1300	
1200	
1100	Apparent dormant interval of 400-500 years
1000	
900	Tephra eruption
800	
700	
600	Apparent dormant interval of 400-500 years
500	
400	Tephra eruptions, mudflows
300	
200	Tephra eruptions
A.D. 100	Lava flows
0	
	Pyroclastic flows, mudflows
B.C. 100	
	Pyroclastic flows
200	
300	Pyroclastic flows, tephra eruptions, mudflows Tephra eruptions, mudflows Lava flows
400	
SCALE CHANGE 500	Apparent dormant interval of 400-500 years
	Repeated eruption of large pyroclastic flows, domes, and tephra; mudflows
1000	
	Apparent dormant interval of ca. 400 years
1500	Intermittent tephra eruptions of large volume, pyroclastic flows, eruptions of domes; mudflows
2000	
B.C. 2500	Apparent dormant interval of 4000 years

flows all make sense in modern terms, but what is significant is that there has *never* been a reported fatality related to an eruption at this volcano. Would that it had been so in 1980. As this is being written there are a known twenty-four persons dead and a reported forty-five to fifty-five persons still missing. It is entirely possible that some of these people will never be found. Further, there is the incalcuable long-range effect of the continued inhalation of the ash fallout . . . respiratory problems or something far worse? We have simply never experienced anything like this before, and the ash which fell as far as Montana to the east and Tacoma and Eugene, Oregon, to the west and northwest may one day prove to be something far more ominous than the temporary plagues of darkness which afflicted some communities.

Still destruction and damage is also of such incalcuable magnitude and their effect is far-reaching enough to merit the position that the events of May 18 and afterward belong in those chronicles devoted to our nations darkest hours.

In the immediate area of the eruptions unknown quantities of wildlife, including millions of fish, were destroyed. When the waters of the Toutle River rose from their normal 50 degrees to nearly 90 degrees due to the boiling mud, fish were actually seen leaping to the shore. An estimate of the salmon and trout that died in the river and several state hatcheries also engulfed by the mudflows runs as high as 70 million, but this did not include the fish surviving the mud and heat — though perhaps not the deadly volcanic ash with its silica content. These jagged, microscopic glass particles would clog or slit their gills thus insuring the prediction of one expert from the Washington State Department of Fisheries: "It will be a long time before the Toutle will be a viable habitat if it ever will."

Other aspects of nature were also thrown into an upheaval, almost obliterated, putting the precious balance of nature into a new rebuilding program. Some of this scarred area may never be the same. Spirit Lake, which was built as a result of volcanic process, scarcely exists today and will surely take a considerable period to be reborn again as the lovely body of water facing the then lovely, now gnarled, mountain above it. It could have been far, far worse: the natural dam formed of ash, earth, mud and felled timber at the outlet of the lake raised the water level, which in turn threatened to break through and swamp the Toutle Valley and the cities of Kelso and Longview. Although some 50,000 of the residents of the area were alerted for possible evacuation, the new dam held and authorities called off the emergency alert.

The outpouring of volcanic ash far beyond the immediate area was a crucial if not critical problem. Areas of eastern Washington, northern Idaho, and western Montana were afflicted with 60,000 tons of gritty ash-dust, which was measured on the ground in levels ranging from less than one inch to six inches. Cities were shut down, the result — virtually impossible traffic conditions. The fear of air pollution and the claustrophobic pyschological conditions imposed by the darkness resulted from ash fallout. Fortunately, no city or town was impaired by these conditions for more than a few days, but the long-range physical effects simply cannot be predicted with any degree of accuracy. Lost business and short term psychological damage pale before this possibility, significant though it may be.

"When the top of Mt. St. Helens blew off, it changed the skyline of the Pacific Coast and the landscape of western Montana," begins the newspaper account of Kevin Miller, staff writer of the Missoula, Montana, *Missoulian*. Yet the citizens of this city of 60,000 situated approximately 400 miles away from the site of Mt. St. Helens had not given much serious thought to their own participation in the great drama that was about to unfold.

"The idea of it settled on the mind about as slowly and subtly as the first ash began sifting out of the sky and falling towards us Sunday night," Miller later recalled. "This greyish, powdery geological junk, the innards of a mountain, was going to stay with us for many days. It would change our lives for much of that time driving home the point that we are still very much at the mercy of the elements."

"As the ash began falling heavily like thick powdered snow, we didn't know whether it was corrosive, abrasive, toxic, or harmless," wrote Miller. "There was no panic, though, because somewhere deep inside us was a strongly rooted assurance that if something really nasty was about to set upon us the authorities would warn us. As it turned out, at least for awhile, we were just lucky because they didn't know anymore about it than we did. It wasn't until late that night that a general warning was given the citizenry of Missoula. Wear masks. Do not attempt to travel. No school. In fact, no anything apart from vital services.

Waking up in the morning and first viewing the eerie sight outside his window, Miller was reminded of some of his favorite fiction. "One of the standard openings for a science fiction story is the wayward traveller's discovery of a dead city where buildings remain standing but nothing moves," he was to recall. "Anyone who woke up early on Monday morning and took a long look at Missoula witnessed a disturbingly real looking version of that scene. It was a sight that stuck in the mind, the kind of memory that becomes a backdrop for nightmares."

Still and all things didn't seem all that bad. Missoula wasn't like Yakima, for instance, where the dust was so deep that snow plows were being called in to deal with it. "We were close enough to the mountain to be bonafide participants of the Mt. St. Helens eruption, but far enough away so we didn't have to endure the long term hardships that will plague our neighbors to the west for weeks and maybe months."

Business losses were huge, however, throughout the area and the pyschology of economic loss is no slight matter nor is the fear, distress, and great inconvenience caused to thousands of people. Airports were closed and thousands of land vehicles, including trains, were also grounded by the storms of ash-dust. So much mud found its way into one stretch of the Columbia River, normally wide enough for ocean going vessels, that the passage shrank to a mere 14 feet in depth and 200 feet in width — one third its normal size — trapping 30-plus ocean-going ships in Portland, Oregon and Vancouver, Washington. To some degree or other much of the area simply stopped functioning.

Not only were bridges and roads destroyed, countless others were made impassable for a considerable period of time, more than 6,000 miles of local roads and state highways just in the State of Washington. An estimate of road damage in Southeast Washington comes to tens of millions of dollars. A single state highway, which ran parallel to the Toutle River, sustained damage in excess of fifty million dollars. Seven of the eight bridges along a twenty mile stretch of this highway were destroyed by mudslides and it will take months, perhaps years, before all the roads and bridges in the area are restored or repaired.

Quite apart from Spirit Lake, the damage to the Cowlitz and Columbia Rivers was nothing less than immense. The Corps of Engineers estimated that between five million and ten million yards of mud had flowed down the Cowlitz into the Columbia River and that just dredging it alone will take as long as a year and cost upwards of fifteen million dollars.

Although agricultural experts at first predicted that the plague of ash might be endangering the soil of the area, there seemed to be reassuring evidence that the acidity of ash dust was not a dangerous factor. There was even speculation that the ash might actually fertilize the ground because of its high amounts of magnesium, calcium, and other useful trace metals. This may prove to be so, but the silica content must also be considered. These hard, glassy particles might take generations to break down and no one can predict when the silica could be of any nutrient value to the ground, agriculture or plant life, not to mention the various forms of animals and insect life inhabiting or reinhabiting the area. There are rumors already that skunk cabbage, as persistent and indomitable as human beings, has begun to return. As of this writing, however, those rumors are unconfirmed.

When the eruptions of the Memorial Day weekend were over, the official government estimate of the loss to crops, timber, and property had risen to nearly 1.5 billion and the figure would grow as damage continued with the further eruptions in mid-June. Such a dollar figure, staggering as it might be, still cannot incorproate all the intangibles involved in such an event as Mt. St. Helens. This estimate does not include, for instance, the losses in Washington State alone to 370,000 people who had been left unemployed as a result of the ravages of nature. Many of these people returned to their jobs within a reasonable period of time, but an estimated 10% probably will never regain their former employment.

In the midst of these high volcanic dramas, the deaths and births of mountains, comes mankind embellishing the story. The myth-making urge has always been with us. Fiction continues to blend with fact, rumors continue to influence our reality and we end by creating our own dramas, our own heroes. Even before his death on May 18th, Harry Truman, manager of Spirit Lake Lodge, had attained the rank of a legend. A glorious example of the absurd and irrepressible courage found in the human species. This is in part what legends and heroes can do for us. They raise our kind up a bit and diminish a little the awesome gap between us and those natural forces beyond our control. We look for the account which puts us in the best light. We create our own adventures and with the remarkable recovery that belongs to the race we turn to jokes: "Why did Mt. St. Helens erupt?" "She forgot to take her Earth control pill."

The ash jokes are particularly rampant today in and around the Mt. St. Helens area. We hear repeatedly that Mt. St. Helens has "made an ash out of herself" and those who won't clean their sidewalks are asked "Are you going to sit there on your ash and do nothing?"

Some are more spontaneous, "I couldn't join another committee," one geology professor was overheard to say, "I'm up to my ears in Mt. St. Helens." "Don't you mean up to your ash?", the colleague responded.

So it goes, a little disrespect for that which we fear, or a humanizing story, a legend, an embellishment, anything that gives us back a semblance of control and allows us to cope with our sorely threatened loss of importance, all these are welcome.

The gags are, verbal, visual, and continual. Washington state car owners have altered their license plates to read "Ashington — the Volcano State." Today on the street a new art form is emerging, dust mask decorations. Wearing dust masks has become a way of life in many cities surrounding the Mt. St. Helens area. Colorful lips and gleaming teeth in fixed, but cheerful, smiles have begun to spread over the sterile white surfaces of these protective masks. Another example of human ability to bounce back and make the best of a situation they cannot control.

The cost of Mt. St. Helens in humanistic terms is a long way from fitting comfortably into any official figure. In truth, some calculations defy the ability of man to measure them much as the volcano itself defies the best efforts of scientists to predict whether it would erupt at all this past Spring and just when the shattering event would take place.

If any or all of the above suggests that the best scientific minds have not been applied to the task at hand, that is simply not the case. In point of fact, there existed a very comprehensive scenario of what might happen if Mt. St. Helens erupted — complete with predictions of when the event might take place. It makes for fascinating reading. The following material is excerpted from a 1978 U.S. Government document, *Potential Hazards from Future Eruptions of Mt. St. Helens, Volcano, Washington*. The work of Dwight R. Crandell and Donal R. Mullineaux, an expansion on the previous work of other scientists, it combines scientific objectivity with the slightly morbid appeal of a disaster movie, although that surely was not the authors intent.

Following this material Dr. Palmer reviews the actuality of Mt. St. Helens' eruptions in the light of these predictions made two years earlier. How many of them came to pass? We know that we have experienced what has been, with no fear of exaggeration or hyperbole, a national disaster, but in the Biblical sense, do we also have cause to count our blessings?

First, the 1978 Government document:

"Mount St. Helens is a symmetrical volcanic cone in southwestern Washington about 75 km northeast of Portland, Oregon. Most of the visible part of the cone has been formed within the last thousand years, but it overlies an older volcanic center that evidently came into existence before 36,000 years ago (Hyde, 1975). Mount St. Helens has had a long history of spasmodic explosive activity, and we believe it to be an especially dangerous volcano because of its past behavior and the relatively high frequency of its eruptions during the last 4,500 years. In the future, Mount St. Helens probably will erupt violently and intermittently just as it has in the recent geological past, and these future eruptions will affect human life and health, property, agriculture, and general economic welfare over a broad area.

PRODUCTS OF ERUPTIONS AND ASSOCIATED HAZARDS

"Future eruptions probably will produce lava flows, domes, tephra (pumice and other airborne rock debris), and pyroclastic flows, most of which will be accompanied by the emission of gases; some of these eruptions may cause mudflows to be formed."

LAVA FLOWS

"The quiet eruption of hot, relatively fluid molten rock (lava) forms lava flows; flows move downslope away from their source vents until the lava cools and solidifies. Typically, lava from volcanoes like Mount St. Helens appears only after an eruption has been in progress for days or weeks, rather than during the first part of the eruption.

"Future flows at Mount St. Helens like those of the recent past probably will be erupted from vents on the flanks of the volcano, because the large dome that forms the summit is likely to divert rising magma to the volcano's flanks. Flank eruptions will affect only the areas that are downslope from vents, and the paths of flows can thus be anticipated shortly after an eruption begins. Based on the extent of most previous lava flows at Mount St. Helens, future flows probably will not extend more than about 5 km beyond the base of the volcano and few will reach beyond the volcano's flanks.

"Motion pictures of lava moving at a high speed have given rise to the common misconception that lava flows move forward so rapidly that people cannot escape; however, lava rarely moves rapidly unless it is flowing down a steep slope along a well-established channel. The fronts of lava flows usually advance at rates ranging from those which are barely perceptible to about as fast as a person can walk.

"Although lava flows present relatively little direct danger to human life, those that extend into and melt deep snow could cause destructive floods and mudflows. Elsewhere, lava moving into a forest could start fires.

DOMES

"Volcanic domes are masses of solid rock that are formed when stiff, pasty lava erupted from a volcanic vent is so viscous that it extends as far upward as outward, and forms a mushroom-shaped cap over the vent. A lava flow will result if the molten rock is fluid enough to move sideways from the vent over the surface of the ground, and gradations exist between lava flows and domes. The sides of domes are typically steep and very unstable and commonly collapse during or shortly after formation. Domes may also be partly destroyed by explosions.

"Domes, like lava flows, usually are formed after other kinds of activity have occurred and are generally erupted even more slowly than lava flows. Because of the presence of the summit dome most future domes at Mount St. Helens probably will be erupted from vents on the flanks of the volcano, like the Goat Rocks dome. The direct effects of a dome eruption would be confined to nearby areas; they would include destruction of the preexisting surface, burial of closely adjacent areas by rock debris, and possibly forest fires started by hot rock fragments.

"A greater danger, however, exists from the associated indirect effects. For example, explosions can cause large rockfalls from the flanks of domes, and these, in turn, may become swiftly moving avalanches of rock debris. Explosions can also cause lateral blasts of great force which can carry steam and rock fragments from the dome outward at a high speed to distances of at least 10 km. Pyroclastic flows, rock-debris avalanches, and mudflows associated with the dome eruption could affect areas much further away.

TEPHRA

"Tephra is the term used in this report to describe particles of molten or solid rock of any size that are erupted into the air above a volcano. Eruptions that produce tephra may range from explosively rapid, continuous rushes of fragment-laden gas that continue for hours, to blasts that last only a few seconds. Most explosions are directed upward at high angles, but some are directed laterally at low angles."

"A tephra eruption can occur suddenly and be the first or one of the first events of an eruptive episode. Very large volumes of tephra generally are not produced at the outset of an eruption, but may be ejected within a few hours or a few days."

"Future tephra eruptions are possible from vents on any flank of Mount St. Helens, as well as from the summit, and thus any part of the volcano can be affected.

"Tephra endangers lives and property by the impact of flying fragments, by forming a blanket covering the ground surface, by producing a suspension of fine particles in air and water, by carrying acids, and, close to the vent, by its heat. People can be injured by falling fragments, by breathing tephra-contaminated air, by collapse of tephra-laden roofs, and by fires started by hot fragments. Tephra eruptions can also result in psychological stresses by blocking roads and causing people to be isolated, by causing darkness during daylight hours, by increasing acidity and turbidity in exposed water supplies, and by interrupting telephone, radio, and electrical services. Exposure to one or more of these stresses may lead to panic even though an individual's health or life is not directly endangered. Damage to property results largely from the weight of tephra, especially if it becomes water soaked, from its smothering effect, from abrasion, and from corrosion. Machinery is especially susceptible to the last two effects. The health and economic welfare of people in the fallout area can also be radically affected by the destruction of or damage to food crops and domesticated animals.

"Hazards from tephra decrease rapidly in severity downwind, so that beyond a distance of 25-30 km tephra from most eruptions is more likely to cause maintenance and clean-up problems than to present a direct hazard to human life. However, even small amounts of tephra falling for a period of weeks or months can have serious cumulative effects on health and economic welfare.

VOLCANIC GASES

"Volcanoes emit gases, sometimes alone, sometimes in conjunction with the eruption of molten or solid rock materials. Gases erupted under great pressure generally carry some rock material, but quiet emission of gas alone is common. Gases emitted by volcanoes consist chiefly of water vapor, carbon dioxide, carbon monoxide, and various compounds of sulfur, chlorine, and nitrogen; some volcanoes also emit fluorine. Many eruptions begin and end with gas emission, but discharge of gases does not necessarily signify that an eruption is about to begin, nor does it invariably occur before an eruption.

"Quietly emitted gases may be concentrated and "strong" near a vent, but usually disperse rapidly and become diluted downwind. Distribution of the gases is mostly controlled by wind, and dilute gas odors have been reported many tens of kilometers downwind from erupting vents. Explosively erupted gases may be driven laterally away from a vent at high speed, but they quickly lose force, and then drift and disperse.

"Volcanic gases can be dangerous to health or life as well as to property (Wilcox, 1959). Gases are potentially injurious to people mainly because of the effects of acid and ammonia compounds on eyes and respiratory systems, and they may also have other adverse effects. Enough carbon dioxide and carbon monoxide can collect in local basins to suffocate unwary animals or people. Gases can harm plants and can poison animals that eat the plants; they also can corrode metal. Cumulative effects of dilute volcanic gases over a long period may cause substantial property damage.

PYROCLASTIC FLOWS

"Pyroclastic flows are masses of hot, dry rock debris that move like a fluid but that owe their mobility to hot air and other gases mixed with the rock debris. They consist of a coarse basal flow and an accompanying hot dust cloud. Pyroclastic flows can form when large masses of hot rock fragments are suddenly erupted onto the volcano's flanks or when a side of a growing volcanic dome topples or slides outward and downward and shatters into countless fragments of hot rock.

"These masses of hot rock debris can move downslope at high speed owing to the force of gravity, to the force of eruption, or to both. Under favorable conditions they can travel at speeds of 50 to more than 150 kilometers per hour."

"Because of their great mobility, pyroclastic flows can affect areas at considerable distances from the volcano. On the basis of past events at Mount St. Helens, nearly all areas within a distance of 6 km from the base of the volcano could be affected by basal parts of future pyroclastic flows or their accompanying ash clouds; valley floors could be affected for an additional distance of at least 10 km.

"The principal dangers from pyroclastic flows result from (1) the basal flow of hot, relatively coarse rock debris which can bury and incinerate people and objects in its path, and (2) the cloud of hot ash and gases which may accompany the basal flow or occur alone. Such clouds may cause asphyxiation, burning of the lungs by hot dust or steam or other gases, and burning of the skin. In addition, rock fragments carried in the clouds may cause injury by impact, and both impact and heat can damage property.

"The especially severe hazard to human life represented by a pyroclastic flow is due to its great speed and its high temperature. Clouds of hot ash associated with pyroclastic flows that were formed during the 1951 eruption of Mount Lamington, Papua, were hot enough to char wood. One such cloud was estimated to have maintained a temperature of 200° Celsius (C) for a period of 1.5 minutes as it passed a site about 9 km from the volcano (Taylor, 1958). Hot pyroclastic flows produced during that eruption killed 3,000 persons. The cloud from Mount Pelée volcano that devastated St. Pierre, Martinique, in 1902 and killed nearly 30,000 persons is estimated to have had a velocity of at least 160 km/h and a temperature of 700-1,000° C (Macdonald, 1972).

MUDFLOWS

"A mudflow is a mass of water-saturated rock debris, typically containing a wide variety of particle sizes that moves downslope as a fluid under the influence of gravity. During movement, mudflows resemble flowing masses of wet concrete, and because of their fluid nature they generally follow channels and valleys. The rock debris in many volcanic mudflows is derived from masses of loose, unstable material that result from explosive eruptions; water may be provided by rain, melting snow, or the overflow of a crater lake. Mudflows can also be started by lava or a hot pyroclastic flow moving across snow, and can be either hot or cold, depending on the presence or absence of hot rock debris in the mudflow.

"Mudflows can move considerable distances at high speed — some have been reported to travel at speeds as much as 85 km/h."

"Swiftly moving mudflows rise along the

outside of bends in their channels and slop up onto obstacles in their paths. Mudflows of very large volume may overtop streambanks and spread laterally if adjacent surfaces are of low relief.

"The chief danger to human life is that of burial and impact of large boulders carried in mudflows. In addition, mudflows carrying hot rock debris could cause severe burns. Buildings and other structures can be buried, smashed, or removed. Because of their high viscosity and vast carrying power, mudflows can sweep away bridges as well as other massive and heavy structures in their paths. Natural or artificial constrictions in a valley that impede flowage, such as bridges or culverts, cause a mudflow to pond temporarily, deepen, perhaps cover areas that would otherwise not be affected by the mudflow.

"Mudflows from Mount St. Helens contain mostly newly erupted rock debris. These mudflows probably were caused by slides of such rock debris from the flanks of the volcano, or by rapid melting of deep snow by hot pyroclastic flows. If a snowpack were to be melted by a pyroclastic flow, the resulting water could carry a large amount of rock debris derived from the flow itself. If the melting were caused by a lava flow or by a hot ash cloud, the melt water might not carry a large amount of rock debris initially, but torrents racing down slopes, gullies, and valley floors, and eroding loose deposits, would quickly become mudflows, and the total amount of material moving downvalley would thereby greatly increase.

"The absence of an appreciable amount of clay in mudflows from Mount St. Helens suggests that large areas of hydrothermally altered rock did not exist on the volcano in the past, nor are they present today. For this reason, mudflows as large as the largest from Mount Rainier volcano (Crandell, 1971) are not likely to occur in the forseeable future at Mount St. Helens. This conclusion is especially important in relation to the capacity of the reservoirs in the Lewis River valley. For example, the volume of one mudflow from Mount Rainier (at least 2 billion m^3 (Crandell, 1971) is probably more than twice as great as the volume of Swift Reservoir. The vast size of some mudflows from Mount Rainier is attributed to the sliding from the volcano of huge clayey masses of hydrothermally altered rock that probably were already saturated with water and steam at the time of the sliding (Crandell, 1971).

"If a major eruption occurs, one of the greatest potential hazards involves Swift Reservoir. If a volcanic event led directly or indirectly to the failure or overtopping of Swift Dam, a catastrophe could result. A mudflow of very large volume, for example, could raise the level of the reservoir faster than water could be discharged safely. In addition, if such a flow entered the reservoir rapidly, it could create a wave that might overtop the dam if the lake level were high. The Pine Creek and Swift Creek valleys are the two routes by which a mudflow could enter the reservoir. Of these routes, Swift Creek is potentially the most dangerous because of its shorter access route from the volcano to the reservoir.

FLOODS

"The danger presented by flood caused by volcanism is similiar to that of floods of other causes. Those related to volcanism probably will carry unusually large amounts of rock debris, and deposits of sand and gravel many meters thick may result at localities on valley floors where the carrying power of the river decreases for any reason. If a major eruption of Mount St. Helens occurred during a time when the volcano was blanketed by deep snow, and when floods were caused by meteorological conditions, the resulting floods could be higher than normal and could affect valley floors at least as far downstream as the Columbia River.

PREDICTING THE NEXT ERUPTION

"The present dormant state of Mount St. Helens began in 1856, and no way is now known of determining when the volcano will erupt again. Mount St. Helens' behavior pattern during the last 4,500 years has been one of spasmodic periods of activity, separated by five or six dormant intervals of a little more than 2 to 5 centuries' duration. In addition, 12 dormant periods 1 or 2 centuries in length have been identified, and many intervals of a few years or a few decades surely occurred during prolonged periods of intermittent eruptive activity. The volcano's behavior pattern suggests that the quiet interval will not last as long as a thousand years; instead, an eruption is more likely to occur within the next hundred years, and perhaps even before the end of this century."

REFERENCES CITED

Crandell, D.R., 1971, Postglacial lahars from Mount Rainier volcano, Washington: U.S. Geol. Survey Prof. Paper 677, 75 p.

Hyde, J.H., 1975, Upper Pleistocene pyroclastic-flow deposits and lahars south of Mount St. Helens volcano, Washington: U.S. Geol. Survey Bull. 1383-B, 20 p.

Macdonald, G.A., 1972, Volcanoes: Englewood Cliffs, N.J., Prentice-Hall, 510 p.

Taylor, G.A., 1958, The 1951 eruption of Mount Lamington, Papua: Australia Bur. Mineral Resources Geology and Geophysics Bull. 38, 100 p.

Wilcox, R.E., 1959, Some effects of recent volcanic ash falls, with especial reference to Alaska: U.S. Geol. Survey Bull. 1028-N, p. 409-476.

Now That It's Happened

Commentary by Prof. Palmer

The preceding excerpts are a fine example of the value of geological science to society. Crandell, Mullineaux, Hyde, and Hopson have observed, mapped, collected, analyzed, and then predicted with such accuracy that their information, printed two years before the eruption, describes what happened as well as any current report I have seen to date.

If the eruption at Mt. St. Helens was a surprise, it was not for a lack of accurate predictions. It might more likely have been a surprise to the community because scientists tend to write for one another. Perhaps a few "publications" via large, posted signs at hazard sites would add the needed visibility and guide the population toward a higher awareness of the natural hazards of their area. These should include all those potentially hazardous areas where Nature dissipates high amounts of energy, such as river flood plains, beaches struck by tidal waves, and earthquake fault lines.

Basically the information we didn't have on Mt. St. Helens was the kind of data not capable of being documented from volcanic deposits. The past was no help to us here. We need to know much, much more about volcanic earthquakes, high frequency noises, and magnetic variations. Greater knowledge in these areas may help warn us before possible dangerous events occur in the future.

However, I stress *may* because we relearned from this horrendous eruption that for some of Nature's events, there in *no* warning. For many other events scheduled by Nature, the warnings *are* there and it is up to us to learn to read them intelligently and to help our fellow man understand their significance.

The Mt. St. Helens event differed from the prediction by erupting at the summit, producing most of its tephra at the initial blast, and creating an ash cloud which extended beyond the expected limits. Perhaps certain effects of the blasts of the past were simply not recognizable because of the ravages of time, so that no deposit remained to guide the prediction more completely.

Even so, the sites established for observation at Coldwater One and Two appear to be within the mapped ash cloud hazard area. The volcano was no respecter for agency sanction. It treated both official observers and trespassers who were in that area equally.

Eruptive Events of Mt. St. Helens: A Chronology

Mt. St. Helens has progressed through all four stages of eruption during the Spring of 1980. Observations on the dates indicated show the following developments with the beginnings of Stage 4 first sighted June 14th and still in progress.

Stage 1

March 20 First earthquake generated.

March 25-26 Earthquake "storm" with several quakes each hour.

Stage 2 (A)

March 27 Small steam eruption at summit, earthquakes continue.

March 28-29 Cloud cover obscures mountain.

March 30-31 Double craters expand, earthquakes continue.

April 2-6 Summit craters expand, combine into one crater with lobes.

April 8-12 Numerous steam eruptions with plumes of ash and coarse particles ejected from the crater. Landsliding of the crater rim expands crater size. Earthquakes continue at an increasing rate.

April 22 End of first steam eruptive substage after approximately four weeks of eruption.

Stage 2 (B)

April 25 Northward expansion of the north flank of the cone continues more rapidly accompanied by subsidence of the summit crater area.

April 30 Northward expansion and crater subsidence continue at about two feet per day. Sampling and measurement of crater area.

May 4 Expansion of bulge to the North averaging five feet per day. Crater subsidence rapid. Second crater area sampling and measurement.

Stage 2 (C)

May 7 Steam eruptions resume. Northern bulging and crater subsidence continue. Earthquakes continue at progressively decreasing rate. Number and size of larger quakes increases.

May 11-16 North flank is at a critical angle of repose; landsliding is eminent, small slides common. Heat anomalies in bulge area.

Stage 3

May 18 Two magnitude five earthquakes. Landslide of bulge material northward.

0839 A.M. Magmatic eruption blasts eight to ten miles north, 60,000 feet high, wind to E.

1000 A.M. Hot debris flow in South fork of Toutle River.

1400 P.M. Hot debris flow in North fork.

1800 P.M. Plume extends to the Idaho border, eruptive force decreasing, bridges washed out on Toutle River, earthquakes almost absent.

May 19 Eruption subsides, earthquakes much reduced, Columbia River filled twenty-five feet with debris, log jams and muddy water which extends to ocean, rescue operations active.

May 25 Second magmatic eruption, upper wind to WNW, lower winds westward, Portland to Olympia, very little seismicity, rescue operations continue.

May 30-31 Weather clearing, allows view of new crater area. Infrared images show heat in crater and deposits to the North. Spirit Lake filling — hot, water covered with debris.

Early June Occasional eruptions, active fumaroles and steaming, little debris deposited beyond crater.

June 12 Magmatic eruption reported to 40,000 feet; winds SW. 1/8" ash deposits 20 miles SW, 1/16" ash deposits 40 miles SW (Portland).

Stage 4

June 14 First indication of lava dome sighted.

June 18 Lava dome still growing; approximate size as of this date: 280 feet high and 660 feet in diameter. Lava stiff and viscous.

Picture Summary of the Eruption of Mt. St. Helens

174. Small crater develops along with uplift of a thirty-foot peak.

176. Steam blasts emit ice and snow from small crater, scattering ash on the summit.

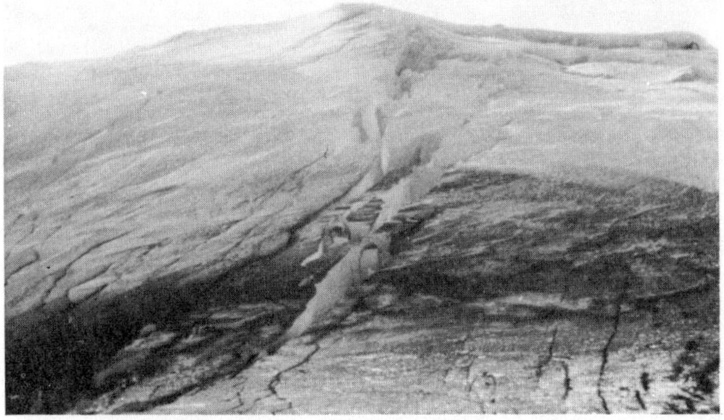

175. Fractures appear on summit area.

177. Second crater develops.

178. Dark ash deposits absorb heat, causing avalanches and ice flows.

179. Cloverleaf pattern formed as a result of craters joining.

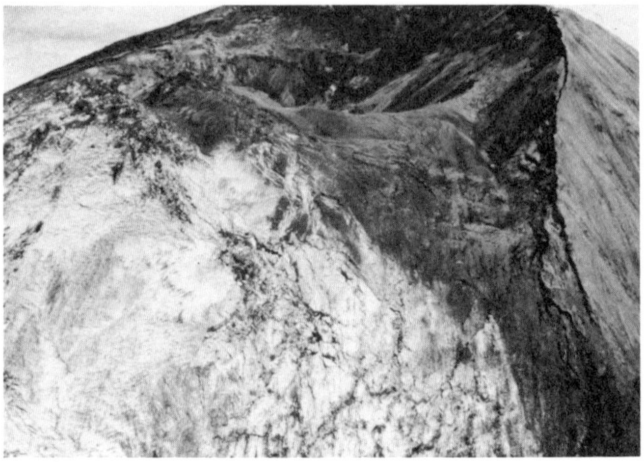

181. New ash continually changes the appearance of the crater area.

180. Ash eruptions continue.

182. By late April a pear-shaped crater formed.

183. Bulge continues to grow, pushing northward, forming a second peak extending about 100 feet upward and outward.

184. A considerable offset between the stable south and the expanding block to the left.

185. Expansion of the bulge had grown to the size of a large dome protruding northward.

186. The mountain explodes!

187. The initial eruptive blast totally devastated the surrounding forest.

188. Explosion caused mudflows and log jams in the Toutle River.

189. Trucks, houses, anything in the way was swamped by the rampaging mud.

190. Rescue missions were activated for possible survivors and then to recover bodies of the dead.

191. The May 18th eruption lowered Mt. St. Helens by over 1,000 feet.

192. Utter devastation where once it was scenic beauty.

193. Magmatic eruption on June 12th, reported at 40,000 feet.

194. Lava dome, looking like dirty cottage cheese, is sighted on June 14th.

195. By June 18, dome had grown to 280 feet high and 660 feet in diameter.

4
A WARNING FOR THE FUTURE

It seems obvious now that the losses at Mt. St. Helens were proportional to the number of people and amount of development present where the volcano released high amounts of energy. Eruptions there, prior to this, had no losses at all, at least in terms of human life. So we *are* fortunate that no greater population had developed near the mountain.

Yet we see continual development in most areas of high energy — violent rivers, dangerous beaches, fault lines, avalanche trails, and landslide areas, to name a few. We build many of our own disasters by usurping the territory better reserved and respected as areas of the natural process. The splendor and fury of high energy areas make them both very hazardous for permanent development and highly interesting to visit.

It seems vital, therefore, that Mt. St. Helens is one of those high risk zones that should be excluded from permanent development and preserved for recreational appreciation. But the residents of the area aren't likely to cheer for this taking place.

The Toutle River Valley floor was *formed* by mudflows, yet the residents are surprised by the latest mudflows. Days turned black, land turned dusty grey and rivers turned to thick, hot, muddy debris — all are a rude surprise for nature-loving residents of the Northwest. Their love for the great outdoors is sorely tested. Anger and frustration give rise to such names as "killer volcano"; calls for bombing the crater; plugging the vent; or the common cry of despair, "It was grand but now I wish it would just go away."

But nature is not subject to government regulations, property boundaries, or product safety liability. The Earth is not so much real estate as it is a resource; not so much property as it is a process. The whole Pacific Northwest is the product of volcanic processes which are still in progress. The mountains, the valleys, the land on which we built our homes and towns is the gift of volcanic processes.

The volcanoes were here thousands of years before us and will be here thousands of years after we are gone. Perhaps that's the object lesson of Mt. St. Helens we ignore at our peril. Somehow we have to learn to enjoy Nature and to co-exist with her. Do we really have any other choice . . . ?

Glossary of Geological Terms

Andesite — Volcanic rock of intermediate composition combining andesine and one or more silicates which gives it a light grey color.

Ash — Uncemented pyroclastic material made up of fragments with a diameter principally under four millimeters.

Basalt — Any dark-color, fine-grained lava, or igneous rock. Plateau basalt refers to those lavas caused by fissure eruptions which spread horizontally over large areas as on the Columbia River Plateau.

Breccia — Pyroclastic rock composed of angular fragments 32 millimeters or more in diameter.

Caldera — A large depression, usually more or less circular and over a mile in diameter, formed either by collapse, explosion or erosion at the summit of a volcano.

Cinders — Uncemented, glassy fragments ranging principally from 2.5 to 4 millimeters in diameter.

Crater — Steep-walled depression, usually in the shape of an inverted cone, found at the summit or on the flanks of a volcano from which volcanic materials are ejected.

Crust — The hard layer of earth which lies above the Mohorovičić seismic discontinuity formed approximately 35 kilometers below continental land masses.

Dacite — An extrusion material principally made up of andesine and quartz.

Dome — A symmetrical, rounded uplift which is normally circular in outline.

Earthquake — A trembling of the earth caused by the sudden release of accumulated pressure.

Fumarole — A vent which issues fumes or gaseous vapors.

Graben — A fairly long narrow block which appears along faults relative to the rocks on each side.

Ground Water — Subsurface phreatic water which is in the saturation zone.

Igneous — Rock formed from the solidification of molten magma.

Lahar — A torrential mud flow or landslide of pyroclastic, usually water-saturated debris down the slope of a volcnao resulting from gravitational forces.

Lava — Fluid rock issued from the vents of a volcano.

Magma — Mobile molten rock together with related gasses, which exists under the crust of the earth.

Metric Equivalent — Kilometer = 0.6 miles; meter = 39.3 inches; millometer = .04 .

Mudflow — Flowage of a great variety of debris mixed with large amounts of water which usually follows established channels or stream-beds.

Nuée Ardente — A French term describing an incandescent, highly heated mass of gas-charged ash which is ejected violently from a volcano and continues at avalanche speed down the side of the mountain.

Phreatic — An extremely violent volcanic explosion caused by the conversion of ground water to steam.

Plate — A section of the earth crust which varies from 50 to 250 kilometers in thickness forming the upper mantel over an inner core of magma.

Pumice — A glassy, extremely cellular lava usually composed of rhyolite.

Pyroclastic — Volcanic material (cinder, pumice, ash, etc.) which has been explosively or aerially ejected from a volcanic vent.

Rhyolite — Rock with crytalline constituents of granite.

Rift Zones — A system of fissures and faults where repeated eruptions occur, usually spreading out from the summit of a volcano.

Seismicity — The likelihood of a particular area being subject to earth movement or vibration. A seismic record is a photograph of reflected or refracted seismic waves or activity.

Silica — Silicone dioxide, most often seen in fine-grained quartz.

Tectonic — Study of the broad structural features of rocks and external forms which result from the change of the earth's crust.

Tephra — A collective term covering all the volcanic ejecta which is spewed from a volcano during an eruption.

Turbidity — Density.

Viscous — A sticky adhesive with a glutinous consistency.

Volcano — A vent in the earth's surface through which pyroclastic ejecta, volcanic gases and lava may issue. Build-up of these materials around the vent forms a mountain.

Epilogue

"There is no way to prepare oneself for the sight that we beheld this morning. I don't know that there's ever been in recorded history in our nation a more formidable explosion. What happened apparently was a natural explosion equivalent maybe to ten megatons of nuclear bombs or ten million tons of TNT that swept across, first with a flash of light and heat 800-1000 degrees, out to a distance of twelve to fifteen miles, that instantly burned everything that was in direct visual sight of the explosion itself.

"This was later followed in two or three minutes by the pressure wave that travels at the speed of sound and that was later followed by this enormous gush of liquid rock and air to some degree with ice that comprised one cubic mile of material. Absolute and total devastation of an area that encompasses about one hundred and fifty miles.

"It's the worst thing I have ever seen. It had been described to me earlier. But it was much worse than the description which had been impressed upon me. I don't know how long it will take for that region to be opened even for normal movement of traffic. There are enormous blocks of ice apparently still covered by literally hundreds of feet of fluffy, face-powder-type ash and as that ice is melted under the hot conditions that exist, enormous cave-ins are taking place. Steam is bubbling up, there are a few fires about.

"Someone said it was like a moonscape, but it's much worse than anything I've ever seen in pictures of the moon's surface. Fortunately, the people in that region were minimal, but it is literally indescribable in its devastation."

— President Jimmy Carter
May 22, 1980

Harry R. Truman
1896 — 1980

"It's definitely a mistake. Somebody done it to cause trouble for me and the law and everybody else . . .

"I have no intentions to leave here — I never had had any intentions and everybody knew it . . .

"The north side has left me alone entirely. I'm on the northeast side. There's no rock, no ash, no nothing on my side. I had some people ask me why the hell I stayed, what I be doing up there. That's my life — Spirit Lake and Mt. St. Helens — my life, folks. I lived there fifty years — it's a part of me. That mountain and that lake is a part of Truman. And I'm a part of it."

May 17, 1980

Harry Truman felt he knew the mountain too well for it to harm him, but he was wrong. His memorial would be the legend he would leave behind.